DISCOVERING AMERICA

Southern New England

CONNECTICUT • MASSACHUSETTS • RHODE ISLAND

By
Thomas G. Aylesworth
Virginia L. Aylesworth

FRANKLIN PIERCE COLLEGE
LIBRARY
RINDGE, NEW HAMPSHIRE

CHELSEA HOUSE PUBLISHERS
New York • Philadelphia

Copyright © 1996 by Chelsea House Publishers, a division of Main Line Book Co. All rights reserved. Printed and bound in Mexico.

First Printing

1 3 5 7 9 8 6 4 2

Library of Congress Cataloging-in-Publication Data

Aylesworth, Thomas G.
Southern New England: Connecticut, Massachusetts, Rhode Island
Thomas G. Aylesworth, Virginia L. Aylesworth.
p. cm.—(Discovering America)
Includes bibliographical references and index.
Summary: Discusses the geographical, historical, and cultural aspects of Connecticut, Massachusetts, and Rhode Island.
ISBN 0-7910-3398-8.
0-7910-3416-X (pbk.)
1. New England—Juvenile literature. 2. Connecticut—Juvenile literature. 3. Massachusetts—Juvenile literature. 4. Rhode Island—Juvenile literature. [1. New England. 2. Connecticut. 3. Massachusetts. 4. Rhode Island.] I. Aylesworth, Virginia L. II. Title. III. Series: Aylesworth, Thomas G. Discovering America.

CNYRR
F4.3.A96 1996 94-45825
974—dc20 CIP
AC

CONTENTS

Connecticut

The state seal dates back to colonial times, but has been modified several times, most recently in 1931. Oval in shape, it has three grapevines in the center that represent the transplanting of the culture and traditions of Europe to the Connecticut colony. Under the vines, a scroll contains the state motto. Around the edge are the words *Sigilium Reipublicae Connecticutensis*, which means "The Seal of the Connecticut Republic" in Latin.

Connecticut also has a state coat of arms. On a white field are the three grapevines bearing their fruit. Under them is a scroll containing the state motto in Gothic script.

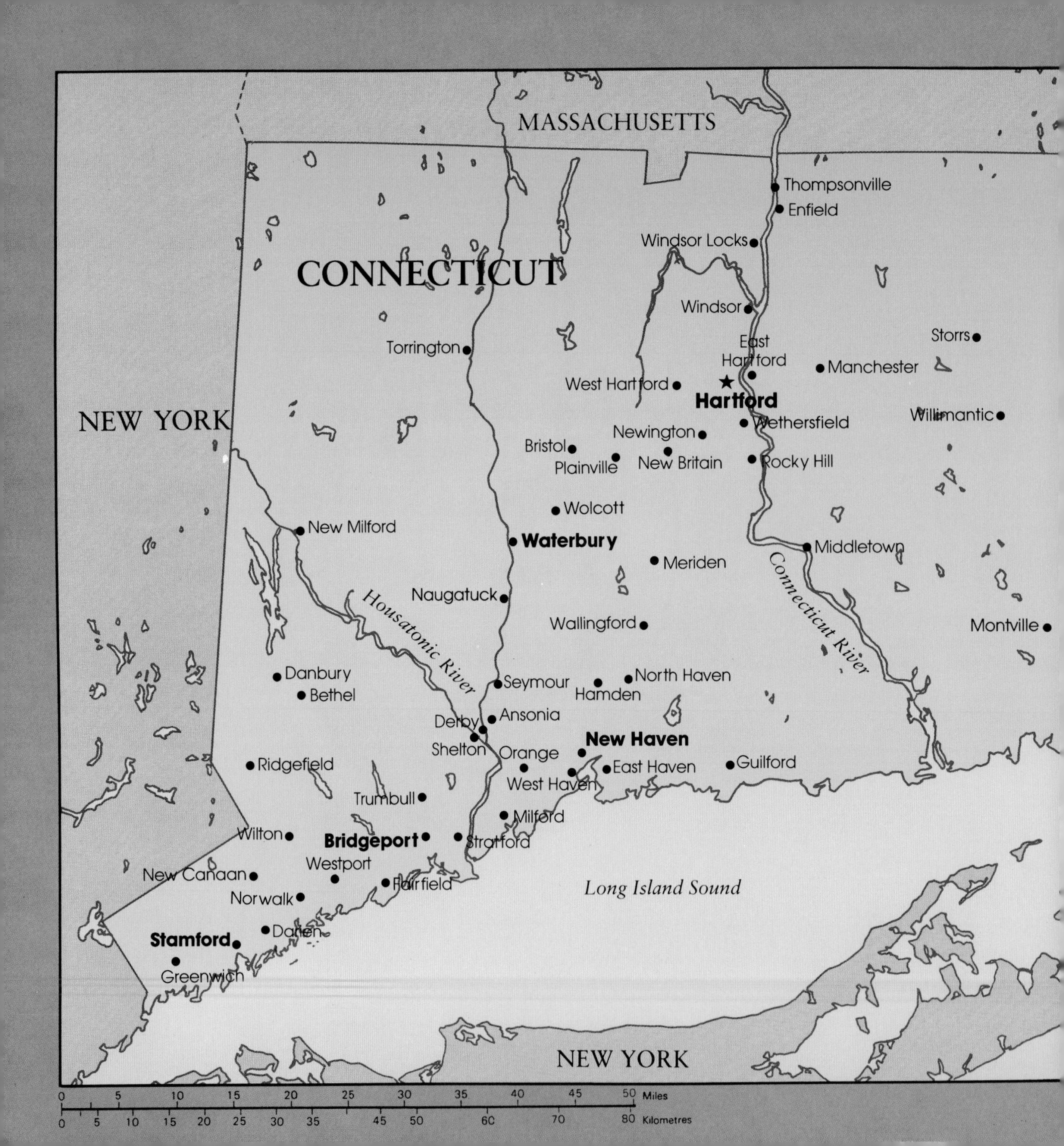
MASSACHUSETTS
CONNECTICUT
NEW YORK
Thompsonville
Enfield
Windsor Locks
Windsor
East Hartford
Storrs
Torrington
Manchester
West Hartford
Hartford
Willimantic
Wethersfield
Newington
Bristol
Plainville
New Britain
Rocky Hill
Wolcott
New Milford
Waterbury
Middletown
Meriden
Connecticut River
Housatonic River
Naugatuck
Wallingford
Montville
Danbury
Bethel
Seymour
North Haven
Hamden
Ansonia
Derby
Shelton
New Haven
Orange
Ridgefield
East Haven
Guilford
West Haven
Trumbull
Milford
Wilton
Bridgeport
Stratford
Westport
New Canaan
Fairfield
Norwalk
Long Island Sound
Darien
Stamford
Greenwich
NEW YORK
0 5 10 15 20 25 30 35 40 45 50 Miles
0 5 10 15 20 25 30 35 45 50 60 70 80 Kilometres

CONNECTICUT

At a Glance

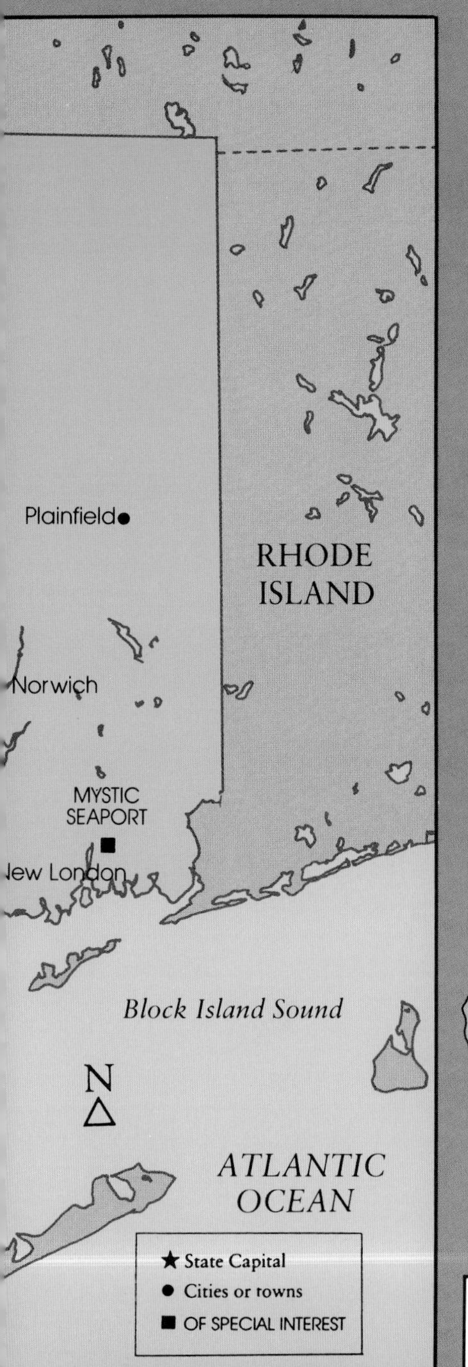

Capital: Hartford

Size: 5,018 square miles (48th largest)
Population: 3,280,959 (27th largest)

Major Industries:
Aircraft engines and parts, submarines, metal products

State Flag

State Bird:
American Robin

The 360 foot cliff of East Rock in New Haven is an unusual geologic formation.

State Flag

The state flag of Connecticut was adopted in 1879, replacing previous flags that dated back to the 1770s. On an azure blue background is a white shield containing the three grapevines and their fruit in natural colors. Under the shield is a white scroll upon which is the state motto.

State Motto

Qui Transtulit Sustinet

The Latin motto, which means "He who transplanted still sustains," was part of the original colonial seal of Connecticut, which also contained a vineyard. It comes from the Bible—verse three of the 79th Psalm.

State Capital

Beginning in 1662, New Haven and Hartford were the twin capitals of Connecticut, but in 1873 Hartford became the sole capital.

State Name and Nicknames

The name *Connecticut* comes from the Indian word "Quinnehtukqut," which means "beside the long tidal river." It is a reference to the Connecticut River, which runs 407 miles from northern New Hampshire to the Long Island Sound.

The official nickname for the state is the "Constitution State," adopted by the legislature in 1959, and it refers to the fact that Connecticut was the first state to have a written constitution. It is also called the "Nutmeg State," not because nutmeg is grown there, but because the old Yankee peddlers from the state sometimes would sell fake nutmegs, carved from wood, to the innocent citizens of the western territories on their selling trips to the frontier.

State Flower

Kalmia latifolia, the mountain laurel, was named the state flower of Connecticut in 1907. Two other names for this flower are "calico bush" and "spoonwood."

State Tree

Quercus alba, the white oak, was named the state tree of Connecticut in 1947. It was selected in remembrance of the Charter Oak, which was the hiding place for the charter given to Connecticut by King Charles II of England in 1662. Twenty-five years later it was repealed by King James II. Certain settlers were determined to hold the rights the charter gave, and so they hid it in a tree.

The mountain laurel is the state flower.

State Bird

The robin, *Turdus migratorius*, became the state bird of Connecticut in 1943.

State Animal

The sperm whale, *Physeter catodon*, was named the state animal of Connecticut in 1979.

State Insect

In 1977 the praying mantis, *Mantis religiosa*, was adopted as the state insect of Connecticut.

State Mineral

The garnet has been the state mineral since 1977.

State Ship
The first nuclear submarine, the U.S.S. *Nautilus*, built in the state, was named the state ship in 1983.

State Song
"Yankee Doodle" was named the state song in 1978. The words were written by Dr. Richard Schuckburgh, and the tune has been traced back to Holland about 1500.

Population
The population of Connecticut in 1992 was 3,280,959, making it the 27th most populous state. There are 671.2 people per square mile.

Industries
The principal industries of the state are manufacturing and trade. The chief products are aircraft engines and parts, submarines, helicopters, bearings, instruments, and electrical equipment. Insurance is one of the chief businesses and is centered in Hartford. The insurance industry was founded at the end of the 18th century when Connecticut began to insure ships and cargoes sailing to the Caribbean.

The Connecticut River, which cuts across the state, has its headwaters in New Hampshire.

Agriculture
The chief crops of the state are tobacco, hay, apples, potatoes, and nursery stock. Connecticut is also a livestock state, and there are estimated to be some 73,000 cattle, 6,800 hogs and pigs, 8,400 sheep, and 5.6 million chickens, geese, and turkeys on its farms. Oak, birch, beech, and maple timber is harvested, and crushed stone and construction sand and gravel are important mineral products. Commercial fishing earned some $62.7 million in 1992.

Government
The governor is elected to a four-year term, as are the lieutenant governor, the attorney general, the comptroller, the secretary of the state, and the state treasurer. The state legislature, or general assembly, which meets from January to June in odd-

numbered years and from February to May in even-numbered years, contains a 36-member senate and a 151-member house of representatives. Voters in each of the 36 senatorial districts elect a senator. The number of representatives varies between 125 and 225 and voters in the state's 169 towns elect either one or two depending on changing population figures. The state constitution was adopted in 1818. In addition to its two U.S. senators, Connecticut has six representatives in the U.S. House of Representatives. The state has eight votes in the electoral college.

A stately white clapboard church on a typical New England village green.

Sports

Collegiate and secondary school sports are played all over the state. The Little League World Series was won by a team from Stamford in 1951, and the title was later captured by Norwalk in 1952 and Windsor Locks in 1965. The team from Trumbull won the 1989 championship. On the professional level, the Hartford Whalers of the National Hockey League play at the Hartford Civic Center.

Major Cities

Hartford (population 139,739). Settled in 1623, Hartford is the capital of the state and is located on the Connecticut River. A major business and manufacturing city, it is the home of more than 50 insurance companies as well as the plants of such giants as Colt Industries, Heublein, and United Technologies. *The Hartford Courant*, founded in 1764, is the oldest continuously published newspaper in the United States.

Things to see in Hartford:
The State Capitol, the Raymond E. Baldwin Museum of Connecticut History, the Butler-McCook Homestead (1782), the Wadsworth Atheneum, the Old State House (1796), the Mark Twain House (1874), the Harriet Beecher Stowe House (1871), the Connecticut Historical Society, Travelers Tower, the Noah Webster Foundation and Historical Society, the Science Museum of Connecticut, Center Church (1807), Bushnell Park, and Elizabeth Park.

New Haven (population 130,474). Settled in 1638, New Haven is a prominent industrial city, and plants of Sargent & Company, Olin, and the Armstrong Rubber Company, among others, are located here. It was here that Eli Whitney invented the principle of interchangeable parts that led to mass production. Noah Webster compiled the first American dictionary here, and Nathan Hale was a student at Yale, the third oldest university in the United States. Northwest of the city is West Rock, a 400-foot sandstone cliff, where three English judges, who had ordered Charles I to be beheaded, took refuge from the soldiers of Charles II in 1661.

Things to see in New Haven: The Yale Art Gallery, the Peabody Museum of Natural History, the Yale Center for British Art, the Green, the Grove Street Cemetery, the New Haven Historical Society Museum, the Pardee-Morris House, Lighthouse Point, the Gowie-Normand House, and the Shore Line Trolley Museum.

Places To Visit

There are 47 state recreation areas in Connecticut.

Branford: Harrison House. Built around 1724, it was restored early in this century.

Bridgeport: Captains Cove Seaport. The H.M.S. *Rose*, a replica of the British warship that inspired the colonists to establish the American Navy during the Revolution, is open to the public.

Bristol: American Clock and Watch Museum. This museum contains more than 1,600 timepieces, plus an exhibit on their history.

Clinton: Stanton House. Built in 1789, this 13-room house is connected to a general store.

Danbury: Scott-Fanton Museum. This establishment includes the Rider House (1785) and the Dodd Hat Shop (1790).

Darien: Bates-Scofield Homestead. This house is a restored 18th-century farmhouse.

East Haddam: Nathan Hale Schoolhouse. This is the one-room school where the Revolutionary patriot taught in 1773.

Essex: Valley Railroad. A steam train which starts in Essex connects with a Connecticut River cruise.

Fairfield: Ogden House. Built around 1750, this building is a saltbox farmhouse.

Farmington: Stanley-Whitman House. Built between 1663 and 1703, this house is one of the finest early 18th-century houses in the United States.

Greenwich: Putnam Cottage Knapp's Tavern. From this tavern, built around 1690, General Israel Putnam made his escape from the British in 1779.

Groton: U.S.S. *Nautilus* Memorial and Submarine Museum. This is the permanent home for the world's first nuclear submarine, and the museum depicts the history of the undersea service.

Guilford: Henry Whitfield House. The oldest stone house in New England, it was built in 1639.

Hadlyme: Gillette Castle State Park. A 184-acre estate once owned by the actor/playwright William Gillette, this park contains his unique 42-room castle.

Litchfield: Tapping Reeve House and Law School. In

this house, built in 1773, the nation's first law school was established in 1784.

Madison: Allis-Bushnell House and Museum. Built about 1789, the house also includes a period doctor's office.

Mystic: Mystic Seaport. This is the country's largest maritime museum and includes old houses, stores, and a whaling ship, a square-rigger, and a fishing schooner.

New London: Monte Cristo Cottage. This is the restored boyhood home of the playwright Eugene O'Neill.

Norwich: Leffingwell Inn. Built in 1675, this inn was the scene of Revolutionary War councils.

Old Saybrook: General William Hart House. Built about 1767, this house was the home of a well-to-do New England politician.

Ridgefield: Keeler Tavern. This inn and stagecoach stop was once a Revolutionary War patriot headquarters.

Southbury: Bullet Hill Schoolhouse. One of the oldest school buildings in the country, it remained in use until 1942. It may predate the Revolution.

Stamford: Stamford Museum and Nature Center. This center contains a New England farm with livestock and a country store, a wildlife center, an observatory, and nature trails.

Storrs: Nathan Hale Homestead. Built by Hale's father in 1776, it also includes a schoolroom.

Stratford: David Judson House and Museum. Built about 1750, the house contains period furnishings.

Wethersfield: Buttolph-Williams House. This restored home was built in 1692.

Windsor: The First Church in Windsor. This United Church of Christ (Congregational) church was built in 1794, but the cemetery dates from 1644.

Windsor Locks: New England Air Museum. One of the largest collections of aircraft and airplane memorabilia in the country, the museum is located next to Bradley International Airport.

Woodbury: Glebe House. Dating from about 1740, this is the house where Samuel Seabury was elected America's first Episcopal bishop in 1783.

Events

There are many events and organizations that schedule activities of various kinds in the state of Connecticut. Here are some of them.

Sports: Balloons over Bristol (Bristol), Ox Ridge Horse Show (Darien), sport car racing at Lime Rock Park (Lakeville), Women's National Rowing Regatta (New Preston), Long Island Sound America Balloon Race (Norwalk), Stafford Motor Speedway (Stafford Springs), Shad Derby Festival (Windsor).

Arts and Crafts: Crafts festivals (Berlin), Essex Art Gallery (Essex), Dogwood Festival (Fairfield), Christmas Crafts Expo (Hartford), Daffodil Festival (Meriden), Art of Northeast USA Exhibition (New Canaan), Rose-Arts Festival (Norwich), Art & Crafts Show (Old Saybrook), Westport Handicrafts Fair (Westport), Antique Dealers Outdoor Show and Sale (Westport).

Music: Goodspeed Opera House (East Haddam), Chamber Arts Festival (Fairfield), Greenwich Philharmonic (Greenwich), Hartford Symphony (Hartford), Summer Chamber Music Festival (Lakeville), Chamber

Music Festival (New Canaan), Schubert Performing Arts Center (New Haven), the Starlight Music Festival of Chamber Music (New Haven), New Haven Symphony (New Haven), Jazz Festival (New Haven), Norfolk Chamber Music Festival (Norfolk), Stamford Chamber Orchestra (Stamford), Stamford Symphony (Stamford), Stamford State Opera (Stamford), Stamford City Ballet (Stamford), Performing Arts (Westport).

Entertainment: Berlin Fair (Berlin), Barnum Festival (Bridgeport), Children's Services Horse Show and Country Fair (Farmington), Taste of Hartford (Hartford), Oyster Festival (Milford), International Space Exploration Festival (New Britain), Main Street, USA (New Britain), Polish Harvest Festival (New Britain), Harbor Festival (New London), Fall Festival (New Preston), Round Hill Scottish Highland Games (Norwalk), Oyster Festival (Norwalk), In-Water Boat Show (Norwalk).

Tours: Chrysanthemum Festival (Bristol), Mountain Laurel Display (Torrington).

Theater: Mertens Theatre (Bridgeport), Downtown Cabaret Theatre (Bridgeport), Darien Dinner Theatre (Darien), Boston Post Road Stage Company (Fairfield), Bushnell Theater (Hartford), Long Wharf Theatre (New Haven), Yale Repertory Theatre (New Haven), UConn Nutmeg Theater (Storrs), Shakespeare Theater (Stratford), Oakdale Musical Theatre (Wallingford), Eugene O'Neill Theater Center (Waterford), Westport Country Playhouse (Westport), Westport Community Theatre (Westport), Performing Arts (Westport).

The beautiful gardens at the Harkness Memorial, near Waterford, are open to the public year round.

Re-enactments of colonial battles and musters occur year-round, bearing witness to the state's heritage.

At right:
Mystic Seaport, on Connecticut's Atlantic shoreline, is one of the state's most historic harbors. During the mid-1800s, it was one of the centers of New England's commercial whaling industry.

Below:
Connecticut has more than 5,000 natural lakes and ponds, the largest of which are Lakes Bantam and Waramaug. Man-made Candlewood Lake, a popular summer resort, was formed by a dam on the Rocky River, a tributary of the Housatonic.

The Land and the Climate

Connecticut is bounded on the west by New York, on the north by Massachusetts, on the east by Rhode Island, and on the south by Long Island Sound. Surprisingly, this small state has five different land regions: the Taconic Section, the Western New England Upland, the Connecticut Valley Lowland, the Eastern New England Upland, and the Coastal Lowland.

The Taconic Section is a small loop in the northwestern corner of Connecticut that extends north into Massachusetts. The highest point in the state—2,380 feet—occurs here on the south slope of Mount Frissell (whose peak is in Massachusetts).

The Western New England Upland covers most of the western third of Connecticut and stretches into Massachusetts and Vermont. It rises from 1,000 to 1,400 feet above sea level, sloping from northwest to southeast. A hilly region with many rivers, it supports dairy and beef cattle. Crops grown here include corn, berries, and vegetables, called truck crops.

At left:
Connecticut's colorful autumn foliage creates a beautiful scene along a country road in Suffield.

Below:
The Coventry area, along the Willimantic River, is a low-lying valley in northeastern Connecticut where corn, hay, cattle and dairy cows are raised.

The Connecticut River, which empties into the Long Island Sound, is the largest in New England. Besides providing a central route through the state, the river is a popular recreation site.

The Connecticut Valley Lowland is a strip of land extending through central Connecticut and into Massachusetts. In this area, which averages 20 miles in width, are lava ridges and low hills. Generally, it follows the broad Connecticut River, and it is a fertile region. Farmers grow potatoes, vegetables, corn, berries, and fruit, and there are some dairy farms.

The Eastern New England Upland covers most of eastern Connecticut and is part of a land formation that extends from Connecticut north to Maine. It is heavily forested, with many river valleys and low hills. This is a fertile region whose crops include corn, tobacco, potatoes, oats, blueberries, and wheat. There are also a good number of poultry farms in the region.

The Coastal Lowlands are part of the region that comprises the whole New England coast. In Connecticut, they extend along a narrow belt on the shores of Long Island Sound. As the name implies, this is low country, with beaches and harbors along the shore. With the exception of Hartford and Waterbury, most of the state's population and industry are concentrated in this strip; there is one town after another from Greenwich to New Haven, with the cities of Bridgeport and Stamford in between.

The shoreline of Connecticut is 618 miles long, if one includes bays and the mouths of numerous rivers. The chief rivers of the state are the Connecticut, the Housatonic, the Naugatuck, the Thames, and the Quinebaug. Tiny as it is, the state contains some 5,000 lakes and ponds.

Connecticut's climate is humid, with rainfall ranging from 42 to 48 inches, scattered throughout the year. Proximity to the sea and the sheltering barrier of the western hills help give Connecticut more moderate temperatures during winter and summer than the rest of New England. Hartford, in the approximate center of the state, has a January average of 26 degrees Fahrenheit and a July average of 73 degrees F. Spring comes earlier, and fall later, than in most of New England. Except for occasional severe winter storms, the climate is moderate year round.

Above:
The sun sets on a beach in Guilford, midway down the Connecticut coast. Hammonasset Point and other nearby beaches are popular recreation centers.

At left:
The Saybrook lighthouse, halfway between New Haven and the Rhode Island border, commands a view of one of the state's best harbors.

The History

Connecticut's original inhabitants were Indians of the Eastern Woodlands. It is estimated that 6,000 to 7,000 of them lived in what would become Connecticut when Europeans arrived in the 17th century. The Indians belonged to several Algonquian tribes, the most powerful of which was the Pequot, who lived in the south along the Thames River, near present-day New London. A branch of the Pequot tribe, the Mahican, lived near what is now the town of Norwich. Other Connecticut tribes were the Niantic, Paugusset, Quinnipiac, Saukiog, Siwanog, Tunxis, and Wangunk.

Connecticut's coast was explored by the Dutchman Adriaen Block in 1614. After sailing inland on the Connecticut River, he claimed the territory for the Netherlands. But the Dutch did not act on this claim until 1633, when they built a small fort—the House of Hope—on the present site of Hartford. This was not followed up by further Dutch colonization.

America's first law school was established at the Tapping Reeve House, in Litchfield, in 1775.

The first permanent settlers in Connecticut were the English, who came down from Massachusetts. They founded Windsor in 1633 and Wethersfield in 1634. Saybrook, Hartford, New Haven, and New London sprang up over the next 12 years. In 1636 Hartford, Wethersfield, and Windsor united to form the Connecticut Colony. Many of these settlers had left Massachusetts in search of greater political and religious freedom. In 1639 the Connecticut Colony adopted the Fundamental Orders as its instrument of government. Based on the liberal ideas of Thomas Hook, a co-founder of Hartford, they provided for a government that embodied the will of the people.

After the displaced Indians were overcome in the Pequot War of 1637, several new towns were established, including Fairfield, Farmington, Middletown, Norwalk, and Stratford. In 1643 the towns of New Haven, Branford, Guilford, Milford, Stamford, and

Southold joined to form the New Haven Colony, so Connecticut now consisted of two colonies—the Connecticut Colony (also called the River Colony) and the New Haven.

The two colonies united in 1665, three years after John Winthrop, Jr., of the Connecticut Colony, received a charter from King Charles II of England granting his colony a strip of land 73 miles wide from Narragansett Bay to the Pacific Ocean. The charter was so liberal in the freedoms it granted that Sir Edmund Andros, governor of the Dominion of New England, tried to seize it in 1687. To save it, citizens reportedly hid it in the great Charter Oak, which once stood in Hartford.

Silas Deane, a native of Groton, was a diplomat during the American Revolution. While practicing law in Wethersfield in 1769, he led opponents of the British Townshend Acts and later represented his home state in the first and second Continental Congresses (1774–76). He was sent to France in 1776 to obtain military supplies and assistance for his countrymen.

Benedict Arnold, born in Norwich, was a heroic Revolutionary War general who later became a traitor. When the Revolution began, Arnold volunteered to help capture much-needed cannons from the British at Fort Ticonderoga with Vermont's Ethan Allen and the Green Mountain Boys. The fort was taken on May 10, 1775, and Arnold went on to fight courageously at Quebec and Lake Champlain. But the Continental Congress promoted other officers to superior rank, and the disappointed Arnold opened secret negotiations with the British. In 1780, in command at West Point, New York, he planned to turn the fort over to the British, but the plot was discovered. Arnold escaped to New York City and led British raids on Virginia and Connecticut. In 1781 he left the country for England, where he died in 1801.

The earliest Connecticut colonists were farmers who raised only enough food for their own needs and usually had to make their own clothing, household utensils, and tools. But gradually, the colony began exporting farm products, especially to the West Indies. Then came manufacturing, and Connecticut became famous for its clocks, brassware, and silver products, which were sold by traveling Yankee peddlers. The people also turned to the sea for their livelihood, and the coastal harbors were full of Connecticut whalers and merchant vessels built in the colony's shipyards during the 1700s.

In the 1760s Great Britain passed a series of laws that antagonized the people of all the colonies. After the Revolutionary War began in Massachusetts in 1775, the majority of Connecticut colonists favored independence from England. Hundreds of Connecticut men joined the patriot forces. Throughout the war, Governor John Trumbull struggled to provide equipment, money, and men for the rebellious colonies. Nathan Hale, a Connecticut man, was hanged by the British for spying, and his dying words won him a lasting place in American history: "I only regret that I have but one life to lose for my country." In 1788 the colony of Connecticut became the fifth state to join the Union.

It was Roger Sherman of Connecticut who broke a deadlock in the Constitutional Convention of 1787. The large states wanted a state's representation to be based on population, and the small states wanted all states to have the same number of delegates to Congress. Sherman came up with the "Connecticut Compromise," which established two houses in Congress—one (the Senate) with equal representation from each state and the other (the House of Representatives) with a membership based on state population.

After the war, Connecticut gave up most of the lands that had been granted in its original charter, keeping only the Western Reserve, now a part of northeastern Ohio. Connecticut sold this tract in 1795 and used the money for education.

By 1840 Connecticut had become a leading industrial state, with a great shortage of labor for its mills and factories. Factory owners sought European labor, and the first large immigrant group came from Ireland. Its descendants represent a substantial proportion of the people of Connecticut today. The second group consisted of Germans—so many of them that their descendants outnumber those of English stock. Then numerous French Canadians arrived to work in the textile mills, followed by Scandinavians, chiefly skilled mechanics and machinists. The final migration into Connecticut was that of the Italians, who settled in growing metropolitan areas.

Connecticut's industrial importance was enhanced by the many inventors who worked in the state. Eli Whitney, best known for his cotton gin, also developed mass-production manufacturing with machine tools that made interchangeable parts, so that one part would fit any device of the same type. Eli Terry of East Hartford began making mass-produced clocks in 1808. Samuel Colt of

New Haven, seen here in 1848, was an important trading center at the beginning of the 19th century. Its busy port brought a great variety of people and goods into Connecticut and made the city one of New England's cultural and commercial capitals.

Statesman Roger Sherman was a signer of the Declaration of Independence, the Articles of Confederation, and the U.S. Constitution. Originally from Massachusetts, Sherman was a shoemaker, farmer, surveyor, and lawyer before he became a merchant and settled in Connecticut for more than 50 years. He served for years in the state legislature and represented Connecticut in Congress.

Hartford invented the repeating pistol and produced firearms of many types in his factory. Charles Goodyear invented a strengthened rubber for industrial use. Connecticut began manufacturing mass-produced goods such as silk, firearms, cigars, shoes, and nuts and bolts.

Transportation also improved in the 19th century. Between 1830 and 1850, 15 railroad companies began operating in the state. Steamships had been serving Connecticut since the early 1800s. Road-building linked once-isolated communities.

When the United States entered World War I in 1917, many of the nation's largest munition plants were operating in Connecticut. More than 67,000 Connecticut men served in the armed forces before the war ended in 1918. The Groton shipyards began to build submarines for the U.S. Navy.

During the Great Depression of the 1930s, Connecticut industry faltered, causing widespread unemployment among factory and mill workers. By then, 90 percent of the population was living in urban areas. But during World War II, the state again became an important supplier of war materials. Airplane engines and propellers, helicopters, shell cases, and submarines were built in great numbers. In 1954 the first atomic submarine, the USS *Nautilus,* was launched from Groton. Aviation-related manufacturing is still a major component of the state's prosperity today, as well as the production of machinery, computer equipment, and pharmaceuticals. Service industries such as real estate, retail and wholesale trade, advertising, and insurance have become quite prosperous; in 1992, service-oriented industries employed 28.3 percent of Connecticut's workers.

Today Connecticut ranks as one of the most prosperous states in the nation—its citizens have the highest average annual income in the country. Cultural life has never been so stimulating, with numerous theater companies, symphony and choral groups, and artists and artisans flourishing statewide.

Yale, in downtown New Haven, is the third oldest university in the country. Founded in 1701 as the Collegiate School, the college was located in Killingworth before it moved to Saybrook in 1707 and then to New Haven in 1716. A sculpture by American artist Alexander Calder sits outside the Beinecke Rare Book and Manuscript Library, pictured above.

Education

Born in West Hartford, Noah Webster was one of our country's foremost lexicographers. After his graduation from Yale and service in the Revolutionary War, he became a schoolteacher. His works include the *Compendious Dictionary of the English Language* (1806) and its larger successor, *An American Dictionary of the English Language* (1828). Webster's spelling books for schoolchildren helped standardize the spelling and pronunciation of American English.

Education has always been important to Connecticut. The first school was founded about 1637 by John Higginson, a teacher and minister. By 1650 a law had been passed that required every town with more than 50 families to have an elementary school; those with more than 100 families were to establish a high school as well. The oldest library in the state, at Yale University in New Haven, dates back to 1701; Yale's Sterling Memorial Library has more than eight million volumes and also houses the Beinecke Rare Book and Manuscript Library—a research haven. Yale is the nation's third oldest university: only Harvard University and the College of William and Mary preceded it.

The first law school in the United States was established at Litchfield and operated between 1784 and 1833. The first free American school for the deaf was established in Hartford in 1817 by Thomas H. Gallaudet.

The People

Approximately 79 percent of "nutmeggers," as residents of Connecticut are known, live in cities and towns, of which Hartford, Bridgeport, New Haven, Waterbury, and Stamford are the largest. Most of the roughly 8.5 percent who were born in foreign countries came from Italy. Roman Catholics make up the state's largest religious body; other prominent religious groups are the Baptists, Episcopalians, Methodists, and members of the United Church of Christ.

Above:
John Brown, who championed the abolition of slavery, was a native of Torrington. Convinced that direct military action was the only way to rid the nation of slavery, Brown and 18 followers attacked and captured the federal arsenal at Harpers Ferry, Virginia (now West Virginia), on October 16, 1859. The survivors were arrested by Colonel Robert E. Lee two days later, and Brown was hanged for treason.

Above:
Although Mark Twain (Samuel Clemens) is best known for his stories of life on the Mississippi River near his home in Hannibal, Missouri, he lived in Hartford for many years. It was during this period that he wrote *The Adventures of Tom Sawyer, The Adventures of Huckleberry Finn,* and other major works.

Famous People
Many famous people were born in the state of Connecticut. Here are a few.

Writers
John Gregory Dunne b.1932, Hartford. Novelist: *True Confessions*
Fitz-Greene Halleck 1790-1867, Guilford. Poet: *Marco Bozzares*
Harriet Mulford Lothrop (Margaret Sidney) 1844-1924, New Haven. Children's novelist: *Five Little Peppers and How They Grew*
Harriet Beecher Stowe 1811-1896, Litchfield. Novelist: *Uncle Tom's Cabin*
Thomas Tryon 1926-91, Hartford. Novelist:. *Harvest Home*
Sloan Wilson b.1920, Norwalk. Novelist: *The Man in the Gray Flannel Suit*

Journalists
Joseph Alsop b.1910, Avon. Syndicated columnist
Stewart Alsop 1914-1974, Avon. Syndicated columnist

Artists
Al Capp 1909-1979, New Haven. Cartoonist: *Li'l Abner*
Frederick Edwin Church 1826-1900, Hartford. Painter of the Hudson River School

Born and educated in Connecticut, Harriet Beecher Stowe had only a limited personal experience with slavery. However, her 1851 novel, Uncle Tom's Cabin, *cut to the heart of the issue and fueled the abolitionist movement.*

Frederick Law Olmstead 1822-1903, Hartford. Landscape architect
John Trumbull 1756-1843, Lebanon. Painter

Singers
Karen Carpenter 1950-1983, New Haven. Pop-rock singer
Richard Carpenter b.1946, New Haven. Pop-rock singer
Gene Pitney b.1941, Hartford. Rock composer and pop singer

Producers and Directors
Norman Lear b.1922, New Haven. Television producer and director: *All in the Family*
Grant Tinker b.1926, Stamford. Television producer and network executive

Other Entertainers
P. T. Barnum 1810-1891, Bethel. Showman and circus owner
Jerry Bock b.1928, New Haven. Broadway

composer: *Fiddler on the Roof*

Harold Rome b.1908, Hartford. Broadway composer: *Fanny*

Classical Musicians

Eileen Farrell b.1920, Willimantic. Operatic soprano

Charles Ives 1874-1954, Danbury. Pulitzer Prize-winning composer

Rosa Ponselle 1897-1981, Meriden. Operatic soprano

Philosophers and Religious Leaders

Amos Bronson Alcott 1799-1888, Wolcott. A philosopher-leader of the New England Transcendentalist group

Jonathan Edwards 1703-1758, East Windsor. Theologian of American Puritanism

William Torrey Harris 1835-1909, Killingly. Philosopher-educator

Scholars

Crane Brinton 1898-1968, Winsted. Historian: *The Anatomy of Revolution*

Noah Webster 1758-1843, West Hartford. Lexicographer: *The American Dictionary of the English Language*

John F. Enders, a pioneer in the field of virus research, contributed work on vaccines to combat measles, polio and other diseases.

Educators

Sarah Porter 1813-1900, Farmington. Founder of Miss Porter's School for Girls

Eleazar Wheelock 1711-1779, Windham. Founder of Dartmouth College

Emma Willard 1787-1870, Berlin. Founder of the Emma Willard School

Scientists and Inventors

William Beaumont 1785-1853, Lebanon. Surgeon: First to study human digestion

David Bushnell 1742-1824, Saybrook. Inventor of the first submarine, *The Turtle*

Samuel Colt 1814-1862, Hartford. Inventor of the Colt revolver

John F. Enders 1897-1986, West Hartford. Nobel Prize-winning microbiologist

John Fitch 1743-1798, Hartford County. Inventor of the first steamboat to carry passengers

Josiah Gibbs 1839-1903, New Haven. Physicist: Founder of thermodynamics and statistical mechanics

Charles Goodyear 1800-1860, New Haven. Inventor of vulcanized rubber
Edward C. Kendall 1886-1972, South Norwalk. Nobel Prize-winning biochemist
Edwin Land b.1909, Bridgeport. Inventor of the instant camera
Benjamin Spock b.1903, New Haven. Pediatrician and author of *Common Sense Book of Baby and Child Care*
John Van Vleck 1899-1980, Middletown. Nobel Prize-winning physicist

Explorer
Nathaniel Palmer 1799-1877, Stonington. First man to sight Antarctica

Government Officials
Dean Acheson 1893-1971, Middletown. Secretary of State under Truman and Pulitzer Prize-winning historian: *Present at the Creation*
Silas Deane 1737-1789, Groton. First American diplomat
Ella T. Grasso 1919-1981, Windsor Locks. First woman elected governor of a state on her own merit, not as a replacement for her husband
Adam Clayton Powell, Jr. 1908-1972, New Haven. Congressman
Abraham Ribicoff b.1910, New Britain. U.S. senator
William Scranton b.1917, Madison. Governor and U.N. ambassador
Jonathan Trumbull 1710-1785, Lebanon. First governor of the state
Oliver Wolcott 1726-1797, Windsor. Governor and signer of the Declaration of Independence

Military Figures
Ethan Allen 1738-1789, Litchfield. Revolutionary War commander of the Green Mountain Boys
Benedict Arnold 1741-1801, Norwich. Revolutionary War general: First a hero and then a traitor
Nathan Hale 1755-1776, Coventry. Revolutionary war hero: hanged by the British as a spy
Isaac Hull 1773-1843, Derby. Commander of the U.S.S. *Constitution* during the War of 1812
William Hull 1753-1825, Derby. General in the War of 1812

Bill Rodgers won both the Boston and New York marathons in the late 1970s.

Social Reformers

Henry Ward Beecher 1813-1887, Litchfield. Leader of the abolition and woman suffrage movements

Lyman Beecher 1775-1863, New Haven. Abolitionist

John Brown 1800-1859, Torrington. Abolitionist: Leader of the raid on Harpers Ferry

Ralph Nader b.1934, Winsted. Consumer advocate

Business Leaders

J. P. Morgan 1837-1913, Hartford. Banker and philanthropist

Eliphalet Remington 1793-1861, Suffield. Rifle manufacturer

George W. Scranton 1811-1861, Madison. Iron manufacturer

Alfred P. Sloan, Jr. 1875-1966, New Haven. President of General Motors

Sports Personalities

Julius Boros b.1920, Fairfield. Champion golfer

Walter Camp 1859-1925, New Britain. Father of American football

Calvin Murphy b.1948, Norwalk. Basketball player

Bill Rodgers b.1947, Hartford. Marathon runner

Bobby Valentine b.1950, Stamford. Major league baseball manager

Actors

Ernest Borgnine b.1917, Hamden. Academy Award-winning actor: *The Dirty Dozen*

Gary Burghoff b.1940, Bristol. Emmy Award-winning television actor: *M*A*S*H*

Glenn Close b.1947, Greenwich. Film actress: *Fatal Attraction, Dangerous Liaisons*

Katharine Hepburn b.1909, Hartford. Four-time Academy Award-winning actress: *The African Queen, On Golden Pond*

Katharine Hepburn is a film legend for her many strong, smart performances.

Ted Knight 1923-1986, Terryville. Emmy Award-winning television actor: *The Mary Tyler Moore Show*

Hope Lange b.1931, Redding Ridge. Television actress: *The Ghost and Mrs. Muir*

Robert Mitchum b.1917, Bridgeport. Film and television actor: *The Winds of War*

Colleges and Universities

There are many colleges and universities in Connecticut. Here are the more prominent, with their locations, dates of founding, and enrollment.

Central Connecticut State University, New Britain, 1849, 10,568

Connecticut College, New London, 1911, 1,978

Eastern Connecticut State University, Willimantic, 1889, 4,475

Fairfield University, Fairfield, 1942, 4,821

Quinnipiac College, Hamden, 1929, 3,405

Sacred Heart University, Bridgeport, 1963, 4,500

Saint Joseph College, West Hartford, 1932, 1,090

Southern Connecticut State University, New Haven, 1893, 13,618

Trinity College, Hartford, 1823, 2,137

United States Coast Guard Academy, New London, 1876, 951

University of Bridgeport, Bridgeport, 1927, 4,278

University of Connecticut, Storrs, 1881, 17,867; *at Hartford,* West Hartford, 1946, 1,294; *at Stamford,* 1951, 1,175

University of Hartford, West Hartford, 1877, 7,743

Wesleyan University, Middletown, 1831, 3,417

Yale University, New Haven, 1701, 10,842

Where To Get More Information

State of Connecticut Department of Economic Development
210 Washington Street
Hartford, CT 06106
1-800-CT-BOUND
1-203-258-4290

Massachusetts

The seal was adopted in 1885 and revised in 1898 and 1971. It is circular, and in the center is the coat of arms of the state, which depicts a gold-colored Indian wearing a shirt, leggings, and moccasins on a blue field. He holds a bow in his right hand and an arrow, pointing downward to symbolize peace, in his left. Over his shoulder is a silver five-pointed star, which represents Massachusetts as a state. Over his head is an arm, a hand, and a sword, referring to the state motto. Below the Indian is a scroll bearing the state motto. Surrounding the circle is a border reading, in Latin, *Sigillum Reipublicae Massachusettensis*, or "Seal of the Commonwealth of Massachusetts."

MASSACHUSETTS
At a Glance

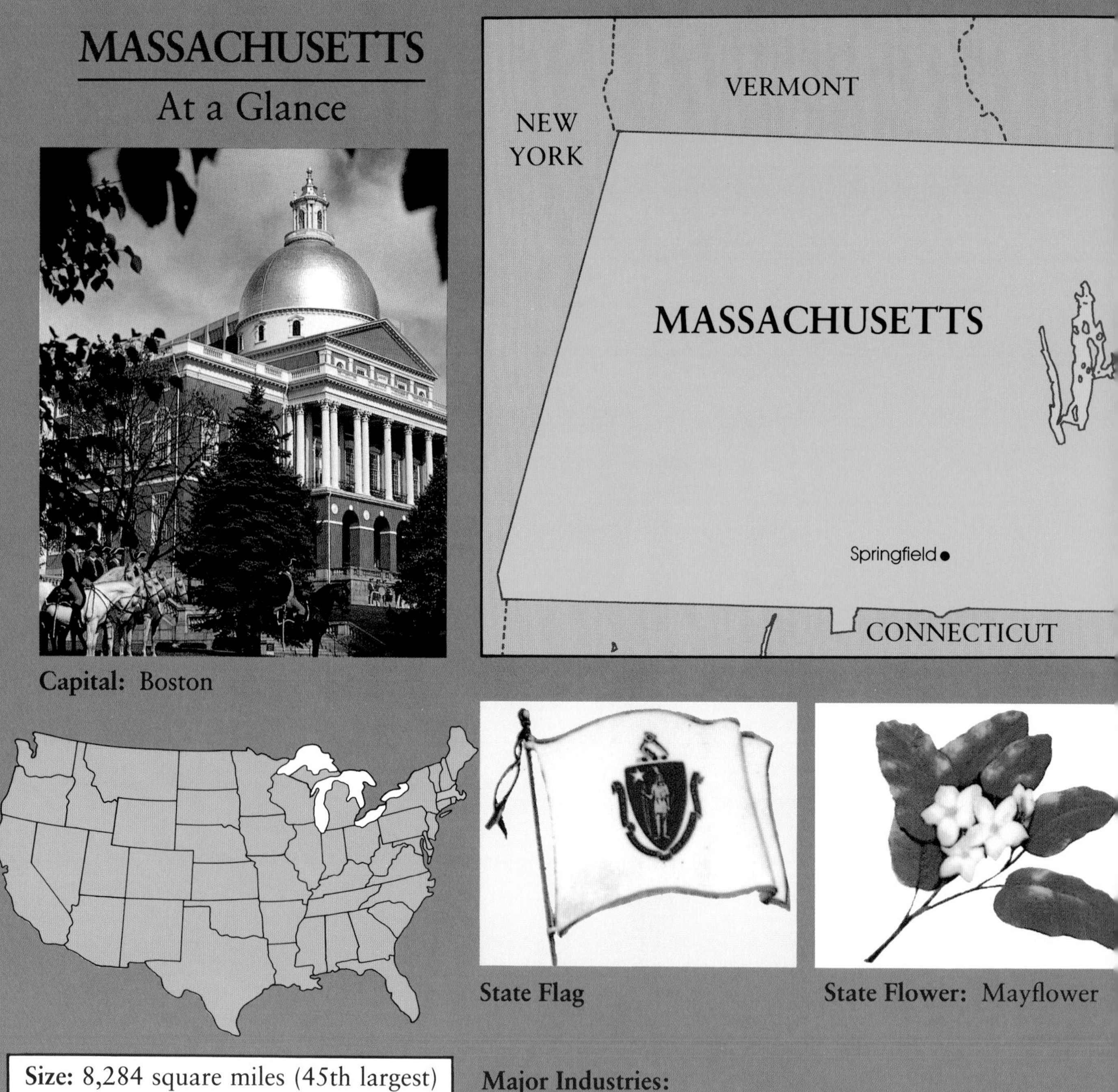

Capital: Boston

State Flag

State Flower: Mayflower

Size: 8,284 square miles (45th largest)
Population: 5,998,375 (13th largest)

Major Industries:
Electronics, machinery, printing, and publishing

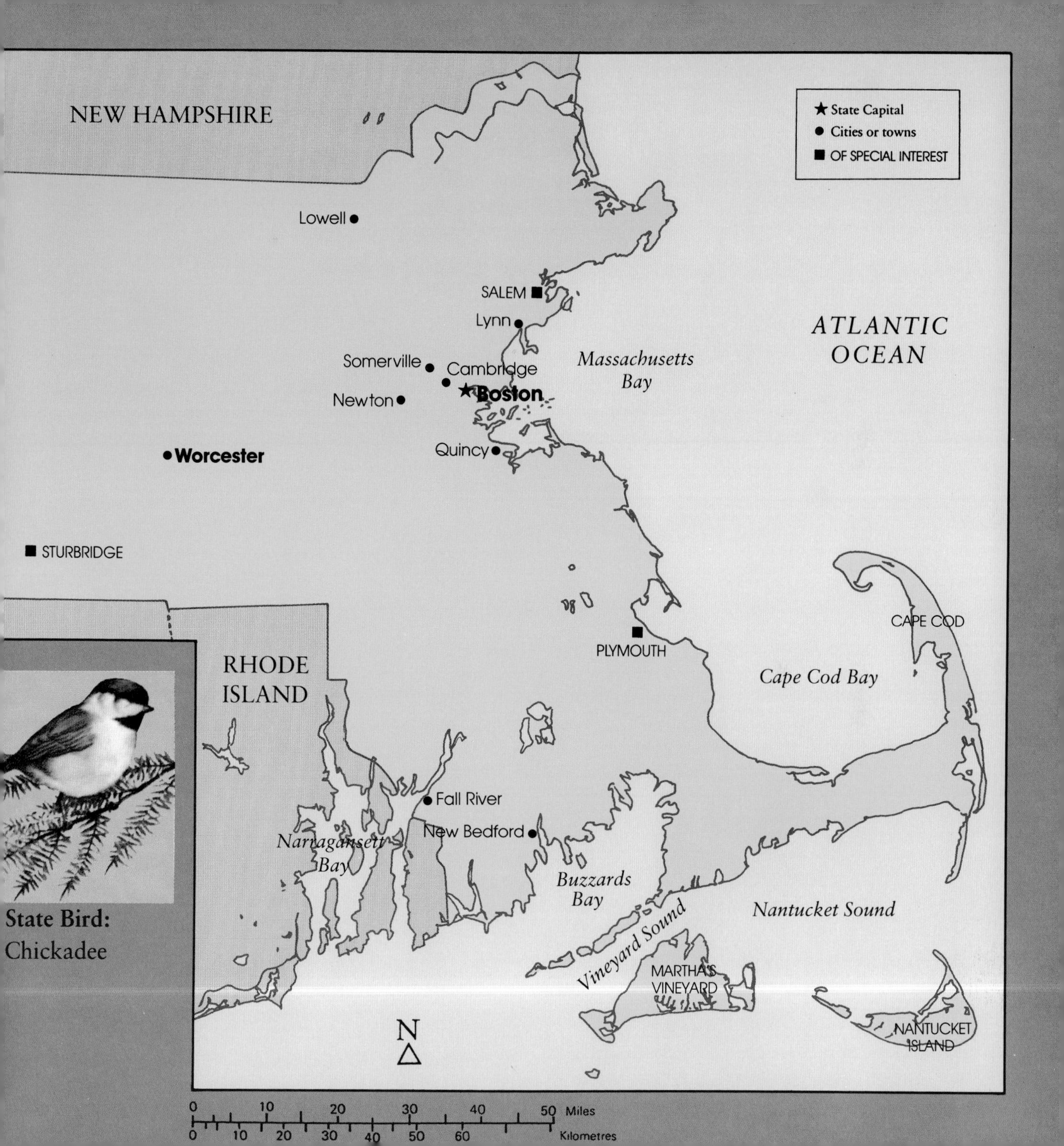

State Bird:
Chickadee

State Flags

The flag of Massachusetts was adopted in 1908. On a white banner the state seal appears in full color. The naval and maritime flag of the state is also white, but with a green pine tree in the center. In 1971 a governor's flag was adopted, which is the same as the state flag except that it is triangular.

State Motto

Ense Petit Placidam sub Libertate Quietem

The translation of the Latin motto is "By the sword we seek peace, but peace only under liberty," and dates back to 1775. It was a quotation from the English Puritan, Algernon Sydney, who wrote it in 1659.

Sunrise over the spruce-covered Berkshire Hills in western Massachusetts.

State Capital

Boston has been the capital of Massachusetts since 1632.

State Name and Nicknames

Massachusetts was named after the Massachusetts Indian tribe. The word *Massachusetts* meant "large hill place" in their language and referred to the Great Blue Hill, which is located south of Milton. Two of its nicknames, the "Bay State" and the "Old Bay State," refer to Massachusetts Bay. Early settlers in the region caused it to be called the "Pilgrim State" and the "Puritan State." The "Old Colony State" is a nickname that recalls the Plymouth Colony, and the "Baked Bean State" refers to the Puritan custom of serving baked beans on Sundays.

State Flower

The mayflower, *Epigea repens*, was adopted by the Commonwealth of Massachusetts in 1918.

State Tree

In 1941 the American elm, *Ulmus americana*, was adopted as the state tree.

State Bird

The state bird of Massachusetts, the chickadee, *Penthestes atricapillus*, was selected in 1941.

State Beverage

Cranberry juice was selected as the state beverage in 1970.

State Stone

Granite was named the state stone in 1983.

State Dog

The Boston terrier was adopted in 1979.

State Fish

In honor of its economic importance, the cod, *Gadus morrhua*, was adopted as state fish in 1974.

State Heroine

Deborah Samson, who fought during the Revolution disguised as a man, was made the state heroine in 1983.

State Rock

The state rock, Roxbury puddingstone, was selected in 1983.

State Fossil

The theropod dinosaur track was selected as state fossil in 1980.

State Historical Rock

Plymouth Rock was named the state historical rock in 1983.

State Insect

The ladybug, or ladybird, *Hippodamia convergens*, was named the state insect in 1974.

State Horse

The Morgan horse was elected state horse in 1970.

State Marine Mammal

Named in 1980, the state marine mammal is the right whale, *Eubalaena glacialis*.

State Gem
Rhodonite was named state gem in 1979.

State Mineral
Babingtonite was named the state mineral in 1981.

State Poem
Adopted in 1981, the state poem is "Blue Hills of Massachusetts," by Katherine E. Mullen.

State Songs
Massachusetts has two state songs, both of them selected in 1981. The commonwealth song is "All Hail to Massachusetts," by Arthur J. Marsh. The commonwealth folk song is "Massachusetts," by Arlo Guthrie.

Population
The population of Massachusetts in 1992 was 5,998,375, making it the 13th most populous state. There are 765.3 people per square mile.

Industries
The principal industries of the state are trade and manufacturing. The chief products are electric and electronic equipment, machinery, printing, and fabricated metal products. Tourism is also an important industry in Massachusetts because of the many historical sites and recreational areas.

Agriculture
The chief crops of the state are cranberries, greenhouse products, nursery plants, and vegetables. Massachusetts is also a livestock state, and there are estimated to be some 120,000 cattle, 50,000 hogs and pigs, 8,000 sheep, 125,000 horses, and 3.6 million chickens, geese, and turkeys on its farms. White pine, oak, and other hardwoods are harvested for lumber, and sand and gravel, crushed stone, and lime are important mineral resources. Commercial fishing earned $280.6 million in 1992.

Government
The governor is elected to a four-year term, as are the lieutenant governor, the secretary of the commonwealth, the treasurer and receiver general, the attorney general, and the state auditor. The state legislature consists of a 40-member Senate and a 160-member House of Representatives. In addition to its two U.S. senators, the Commonwealth of Massachusetts has 11 representatives in the U.S. Congress. The state has 13 votes in the electoral college.

Sports
Many sporting events on the collegiate and secondary school levels are played all over the state. In the 1830s, the Oneida Football Team of Boston was the first soccer team recorded in the United States. Basketball was invented in Springfield in

1891. On the professional level, the Boston Red Sox of the American League play baseball at Fenway Park, and the Celtics of the National Basketball Association play at the Boston Garden, as do the Bruins of the National Hockey League. The New England Patriots of the National Football League play in Sullivan Stadium in Foxboro.

Major Cities

Boston (population 574,283). Settled in 1630, Boston was founded by John Winthrop and his 800 colonists, 200 of whom died during the first winter, mostly of starvation. The American Revolution began here with the Boston Massacre in 1770 and the Boston Tea Party in 1773. The battle of Bunker Hill (June 1775) followed the battles of Lexington and Concord (April 1775).

Things to see in Boston:
The State House (1795), the Park Street Church (1809), the Granary Burying Ground, King's Chapel (1749), the Old Corner Book Store Building (1712), the Old South Meeting House (1729), the Old State House (1713), the site of the Boston Massacre, Faneuil Hall, the Paul Revere House (1680), the Old North Church (1723), Copp's Burying Ground, the Bunker Hill Monument, the U.S.S. *Constitution*, the Nichols House Museum (1804), Louisburg Square, Boston Common, the Central Burying Ground, the Public Garden, Trinity Church (1877), the John Hancock Observatory, the Prudential Center, the Mother Church (The First Church of Christ, Scientist), the Harrison Gray Otis House (1796), the John F. Kennedy National Historic Site, the Royall House (1637), The Children's Museum, the African Meeting House (1806), the Museum of Science, the

Fenway Park, one of the oldest stadiums in the major leagues, is home to the Boston Red Sox.

Boston Tea Party Ship and Museum, the Computer Museum, the Museum at the John Fitzgerald Kennedy Library, the Museum of Fine Arts, the Institute of Contemporary Art, the Isabella Stewart Gardner Museum, the Charles Hayden Planetarium, Bell's Laboratory, the Longyear Museum, the Guild of Boston Artists, the Gibson House Museum, the Boston Aquarium, the Franklin Park Zoo, and the Arnold Arboretum.

Springfield (population 156,983). Settled in 1636 under the leadership of William Pynchon of Springfield, England, Springfield is a major industrial city on the Connecticut River. It is also the city in which basketball was invented in 1891 by Dr. James Naismith.

Things to see in Springfield:
The Springfield Civic Center, Springfield Heritage State Park, the George Walter Vincent Smith Art Museum, the Connecticut Valley Historical Museum, the Museum of Fine Arts, the Science Museum, Storrowton Village, the Laughing Brook Wildlife Sanctuary, the Basketball Hall of Fame, and the Indian Motorcycle Museum.

The U.S.S. Constitution, *nicknamed* Old Ironsides, *was built at the Boston Naval Shipyard in 1794.*

Worcester (population 169,759). Called the "Heart of the Commonwealth," Worcester was settled in 1673. Worcester is the second largest city in New England and is an important industrial center, with some 750 factories.

Things to see in Worcester:
The Worcester Art Museum, the New England Science Center, the Higgins Armory Museum, Salisbury Mansion, the American Antiquarian Society, the Worcester County Horticultural Society, the Craft Center, and Mechanics Hall (1857).

Places To Visit

The National Park Service

Plimoth Plantation is a reconstruction of the Pilgrim colony as it was in 1627.

maintains ten areas in the state of Massachusetts: Minute Man National Historical Park, Longfellow National Historic Site, Adams National Historic Site, Salem Maritime National Historic Site, Saugus Iron Works National Historic Site, Springfield Armory National Historic Site, John F. Kennedy National Historic Site, Boston National Historical Park, Lowell National Historical Park, Dorchester Heights National Historic Site, and Cape Cod National Seashore. In addition, there are 68 state recreation areas.

Amesbury: John Greenleaf Whittier Home. The 19th-century poet lived here for the last 56 years of his life.
Amherst: Emily Dickinson Homestead. This building is the birthplace and home of the poet.
Beverly: Hale House. Built in 1694, Hale House was the home of the Reverend John Hale, active in the Salem witchcraft trials.
Bourne: Aptucxet Trading Post. Here is a replica of a 1627 Pilgrim-Dutch-Indian trading post.
Braintree: General Sylvanus Thayer Birthplace. Built in 1720, this house was the first home of the soldier-educator, who was the superintendent of West Point.
Brewster: Drummer Boy Museum. Set on a 35-acre plot, 21 life-size scenes of the Revolutionary War can be seen.
Cambridge: Christ Church. Built in 1761, this Georgian Colonial building is the oldest church in Cambridge.
Concord: Ralph Waldo Emerson House. The great Transcendental philosopher and essayist lived here for 47 years.
Danvers: Rebecca Nurse Homestead. Built about 1678, this was the home of one of the women executed in the Salem Witch Trials in 1692.
Deerfield: Historic Deerfield. Twelve historic house museums are found in this town, which was twice destroyed by Indian attacks.
Eastham: Old Grist

Windmill. This is the oldest windmill on Cape Cod (1680).

Fall River: Battleship Cove. A World War II submarine, two PT boats, a destroyer, and the battleship U.S.S. *Massachusetts* are anchored here, and many are open to the public.

Haverhill: John Greenleaf Whittier Birthplace. This house is the setting of "Snowbound," Whittier's best known poem.

Hingham: Old Ship Church. This Elizabethan Gothic church has been in continuous use since 1681.

Hyannis: Aqua Circus of Cape Cod. This attraction contains a marine aquarium, a zoo, and a petting zoo.

Lenox: Tanglewood. This was the estate where the writer Nathaniel Hawthorne planned *Tanglewood Tales*. Today it is the summer home of the Boston Symphony Orchestra.

Lexington: Battle Green. The Battle of Lexington, which began the Revolutionary War, was fought on this green by the Minutemen.

Lowell: Whistler House. Built in 1823, this was the birthplace of the painter James Abbott McNeill Whistler.

Lynn: Mary Baker Eddy Historical Home. The founder of the Christian Science Church once lived in this house.

Martha's Vineyard: Oak Bluffs. A series of late 19th-century cottages surround the common of this island community, which began as the site of summer camp meetings.

Nantucket: Whaling Museum. The museum houses an outstanding collection of relics of the whaling industry, from the days when the island was the world's greatest whaling port.

New Bedford: New Bedford Whaling Museum. This museum contains whaling memorabilia and many other types of antiques.

Newburyport: Coffin House. Built in 1654, the Coffin House contains the furnishings of eight generations of people who once lived here.

Pittsfield: Hancock Shaker Village. This village is an original community of the 19th-century religious sect, with 20 restored buildings, including a round stone barn.

Plymouth: Plimoth Plantation. Here is a re-created Pilgrim village, an Indian settlement, and a replica of the *Mayflower*.

Provincetown: Nickerson House. Built in 1746, this unique house was created out of timber from wrecked ships.

Old North Bridge at Concord was the site of one of the first battles of the Revolutionary War.

Quincy: The Adams National Historic Site. This site includes the John Adams and John Quincy Adams birthplaces, the Quincy Homestead, the United First Parish Church, and the Josiah Quincy House in nearby Wollaston.

Salem: House of Seven Gables. This 17th century house, built in 1668, is the setting of Hawthorne's famous novel of the same name.

Sandwich: Heritage Plantation. The plantation includes an antique car exhibit, a military museum, and an art museum.

South Carver: Edaville Railroad and Museum. Here is an old steam train still in use and a 19th-century street of stores.

South Sudbury: Longfellow's Wayside Inn. Built in 1702, this inn was the scene of the poet's *Tales of a Wayside Inn*.

Stockbridge: Norman Rockwell Museum at Stockbridge. This Georgian house contains many paintings by the artist.

Sturbridge: Old Sturbridge Village. This village is a living history museum with more than 40 restored buildings typical of a New England town of the 1830s, all staffed by villagers in period costume demonstrating their crafts.

West Barnstable: West Parish Meetinghouse. Built in 1717, the meetinghouse is the oldest Congregational church in the United States.

Pumpkins, sold at roadside stands and country fairs, have become a symbol of the fall harvest.

Events

There are many events and organizations that schedule activities of various kinds in the state of Massachusetts. Here are some of them.

Sports: Boston Marathon (Boston), Head of the Charles River Regatta (Cambridge), Longsjo Classic Bike Race (Fitchburg), Schooner Festival (Gloucester), The Josh Billings Runaground (Great Barrington to Lenox), Cross-Country Ski Race (Lenox), rowing regattas and Regatta Festival (Lowell), sailing races (Marblehead), Striped Bass and Bluefish Derby (Martha's Vineyard), Sand Castle Contest (Nantucket), Eastern National Morgan Horse Show (Northampton), Quincy Bay Race Week (Quincy), Women's Regatta (South Hadley), Hall of Fame Tip-Off Classic (Springfield), Westfield Canoe Race (Westfield).

Arts and Crafts: Summerthing (Boston), Waterfront Festival (Gloucester), Berkshire Craft Fair (Great Barrington), Antiques Fair (Hyannis), Old Ipswich Days (Ipswich), Cape Cod Antiques Exposition (Orleans), National Amateur Art Festival (Rockport), Crafts Fair (Worcester).

Massachusetts

Tanglewood in western Massachusetts is the summer home of the Boston Symphony Orchestra.

Music: Jacob's Pillow Dance Festival (Beckett), North Shore Music Festival (Beverly), band concerts (Beverly), the Boston Pops (Boston), the Boston Symphony (Boston), the Esplanade Concerts (Boston), Harborfest (Boston), South Shore Music Circus (Cohasset), Band Concerts (Dennis), College Light Opera at Highfield Theatre (Falmouth), Cape Cod Melody Tent (Hyannis), Tanglewood Music Festival (Lenox), South Mountain Concerts (Pittsfield), Summerfest (Quincy), Big Fourth (Springfield), Springfield Symphony (Springfield), Worcester Music Festival (Worcester).

Entertainment: Maple sugaring (Amherst), Sheep Shearing Festival (North Andover), Patriots Day Celebration (Boston), Bunker Hill Day (Boston), First Night Celebration (Boston), Brockton Fair (Brockton), Patriot's Day Parade (Concord), Danvers Family Festival (Danvers), Festival Week (Dennis), Barnstable County Fair (Falmouth), Saint Peter's Fiesta (Gloucester), whale watching (Gloucester), Barrington Fair (Great Barrington), Franklin County Fair (Greenfield), Apple Squeeze Festival (Lenox), Daffodil Weekend (Nantucket), Christmas Stroll (Nantucket), Feast of the Blessed Sacrament (New Bedford), Salmagundi Fair (Newburyport), Yankee Homecoming (Newburyport), Fall Harvest Festival (Newburyport), The Magic of Christmas Present (Newburyport), Fall Foliage Festival (North Adams), Three-County Fair (Northampton), Winter Festival (Northampton), maple sugaring (Northampton), Pilgrim's Progress (Plymouth), Celebration with the Dutch (Plymouth), Thanksgiving Week (Plymouth), Blessing of the Fleet (Provincetown), South Shore Christmas Festival (Quincy), Heritage Festival (Salem), Haunted Happenings (Salem), Cranberry Festival (South Carver), Christmas Festival of Lights (South Carver), Indian Day (Springfield), Glendi Greek Festival (Springfield), Eastern States Exposition (Springfield), Harvest Festival (Stockbridge), New England Thanksgiving (Sturbridge), Re-enactment of the March of Sudbury Minutemen to Concord (Sudbury Center), Fife and Drum Muster and Colonial Fair (Sudbury Center), Westfield Fair (Westfield).

Tours: Beverly Homecoming Week (Beverly), Pairpoint Glassworks (Bourne), Cook's Tour (Hingham), House Tours of Historic Lenox (Lenox), Berkshire Cottages Tours (Lenox).

Theater: Monomoy Theatre (Chatham), Cape Playhouse (Dennis), Falmouth Playhouse (Falmouth), Harwich Junior Theatre (Harwich), Shakespeare & Company (Lenox), Edith Wharton Matinee Plays (Lenox), Academy Playhouse (Orleans), Berkshire Theatre Festival (Stockbridge), Williamstown Theatre Festival (Williamstown).

FERN—ISABEL
EW BEDFORD
ROSIE

Since the *Mayflower* landed at Plymouth Rock in 1620, ships have played a vital role in Massachusetts's history. The settlement around Boston Harbor grew into an international port and a center for trade and shipbuilding; in the 19th century, whaling was also an important industry. Today, commercial fishing and recreational boating continue to enrich the state.

Cranberries are harvested from a bog in Plymouth County, in eastern Massachusetts. The state leads the nation in cranberry production.

The hills and valleys of western Massachusetts are famous for their brilliant displays of fall foliage.

The Land and the Climate

The state of Massachusetts is bounded on the west by New York, on the north by Vermont and New Hampshire, on the east by the Atlantic Ocean, and on the south by Connecticut and Rhode Island. The part of the state that extends to the southeast, ending in Cape Cod, is bounded on the east and south by the Atlantic Ocean and on the west by Rhode Island. Massachusetts has six main land regions. From east to west, they are the Coastal Lowlands, the Eastern New England Upland, the Connecticut Valley Lowland, the Western New England Upland, the Berkshire Valley, and the Taconic Mountains.

The Coastal Lowlands are part of a larger region that makes up the entire New England coastline; they cover the eastern one-third of Massachusetts and include Nantucket Island, Martha's Vineyard, the Elizabeth Islands, and other smaller islands. This is an area of rounded hills, swamps, small lakes, and shallow rivers. The region supports dairy and poultry farms and fruit orchards. Ornamental plants are grown for sale to gardeners and landscapers. Fishing is an important industry along the coast.

The Eastern New England Upland is part of a land formation that extends from Maine to New Jersey. This strip is about 40 to 60 miles wide in Massachusetts, and in parts it rises to about 1,000 feet above sea level, sloping down toward the west. Poultry and dairy cows, fruit, corn, and beef cattle are raised here.

Above:
The lighthouse at Sankaty Head, on Nantucket Island, guides the many fishing boats and other commercial vessels that ply the waters of Nantucket Sound. Fishing has long been an important industry on both Nantucket and Martha's Vineyard, which are popular summer resorts.

At left:
The Berkshire Hills offer numerous opportunities for downhill and cross-country skiing. The scenic mountains of this area can reach an altitude of more than 2,500 feet.

The Connecticut Valley Lowland extends from Connecticut into Massachusetts in a sort of sausage shape. It is only about 20 miles wide, located on the banks of the Connecticut River. The fertile soil supports tobacco, potato, and hay farms, and a healthy maple-syrup industry.

The Western New England Upland is part of a strip that stretches through Vermont, Massachusetts, and Connecticut. It extends 20 to 30 miles westward from the Connecticut Valley Lowland to the Berkshire Valley. This region is the home of the Berkshire Hills, a range of small mountains extending from the Green Mountains of Vermont. Mount Greylock, at 3,491 feet, is the highest point in the state. Hay, corn, fruit, vegetables, and tobacco are grown here, as well as beef and dairy cattle.

Above:
The sun sets over the Berkshire Valley, whose varied foliage and vegetation create a beautiful landscape.

At right:
Rockport, on the northern coast near Cape Ann, relies on the sea for much of its livelihood. Catches in the waters off Massachusetts include flounder, haddock, cod, sea scallops, and lobster.

Above:
Many of the same crops that were raised by colonial farmers are still grown on Old Sturbridge Village land, which supports hay, fruits, corn, squash, and other vegetables.

Above left:
Old Sturbridge Village preserves the ways of New England residents of the early 1800s. Here a sheep is shorn for wool to make clothing and other goods.

The Berkshire Valley is a narrow strip of land that extends into Connecticut. Although it is less than ten miles wide, it is ideal for dairy farming because of its good pasturage.

The Taconic Mountains, on the western edge of Massachusetts, comprise a strip of mountainous land that extends west into New York and north into Vermont. Some limestone is quarried here.

The coastline of Massachusetts is only 192 miles long, but if the shores of the bays and inlets are added, there are more than 1,500 miles of tidal shoreline. The most important rivers in the state are the Connecticut, the Hoosic, the Housatonic, the Blackstone, the Merrimack, and the Taunton. Massachusetts has more than 1,300 lakes.

The climate of Massachusetts, more temperate than that of northern New England, is relatively humid, with an annual rainfall of some 40 to 45 inches, somewhat heavier in summer than in winter. Winter snows are often quite heavy, and snowstorms come on abruptly—sudden weather changes are likely to occur throughout the year. Summer temperatures are often hot. The average January temperature in Boston is 29 degrees Fahrenheit; the average July temperature is 72 degrees F. In the Berkshire Hills, on the western side of the state, both winter and summer temperatures are somewhat lower than along the coast.

Below:
The central Berkshires, along the western section of the state, have been farmed for centuries. This round stone barn is an example of classic Shaker architecture, built by the religious sect that thrived outside Pittsfield from 1781 to 1960.

The *Mayflower II* is docked in the harbor at Plymouth. The ship is a replica of the *Mayflower*, which brought the Pilgrims from Plymouth, England, to Cape Cod Bay in 1620.

The History

It is believed that Indians were living in what would become Massachusetts more than 3,000 years ago. When the Europeans arrived, they found numerous Algonquian Indians, whose tribes included the Massachusett, the Mahican, the Nauset, the Nipmuc, the Pennacook, the Pocomtuc, and the Wampanoag. Many of these Indians were killed by an epidemic of disease in 1616 and 1617; by the time the Pilgrims arrived in 1620, the native population had dropped from about 30,000 to 7,000.

Although European settlement of Massachusetts did not begin until the Pilgrims landed in 1620, the coastal area of the region had been known and explored long before that. It is fairly well established that the Norse—perhaps even Leif Ericson—landed on the Massachusetts coast as early as the year A.D. 1000. The coast may also have been visited by French or Spanish fishermen. It is certain that the English navigator John Cabot arrived in 1498, only six years after Christopher Columbus discovered the New World.

In 1602 the English explorer Bartholomew Gosnold landed on Cuttyhunk Island in the Elizabeth Islands and gave Cape Cod its name. The French explorer Samuel de Champlain drew maps of the coastal region that he had explored in 1606. In 1614 the English captain John Smith sailed along the Massachusetts coast. It was his book, *A Description of New England*, that made the Pilgrims decide to emigrate to Massachusetts.

In the early 1600s, a group of English Protestants had broken away from the Church of England, but they were not permitted to worship in their own way. In order to gain religious freedom, more than 100 of them decided to sail to the unknown wilds of Massachusetts in 1620. They saw this journey as a religious pilgrimage, and called themselves the Pilgrims. Sailing from Plymouth, England, on September 16, 1620, they arrived in what is now Provincetown Harbor that November. Before leaving their ship, the *Mayflower*, they drew up a plan of self-government called the Mayflower Compact. Then they sailed across Cape Cod Bay and founded the community of Plymouth in December. This was the first permanent New World settlement north of Virginia.

The first winter was murderous because no crops had been raised: the only food the settlers could find was the game that they killed. The bark shelters they built were little protection against the cold. About half of them died that winter. But soon the Pilgrims became friendly with the local Indians, the Wampanoag, who taught them to plant corn and beans, which meant that they would have enough food to last through the next winter. The Pilgrims held the first Thanksgiving in 1621, in gratitude for their deliverance from hunger.

John Winthrop, a London lawyer, and his group called the Puritans, were granted a charter by King Charles I of England in 1629. The charter gave them the right to set up an English settlement in the Massachusetts Bay area. Winthrop and about 300 Puritans set sail, and when they arrived in the New World, they joined a settlement that had been established in Salem about three years before. In 1630, the Puritans left Salem and began a settlement which

This engraving, etched and printed by Boston's Paul Revere, shows British ships landing in Boston Harbor in 1768. British troops established a presence in the city to enforce the import taxes placed on various items by the Townshend Acts of 1767.

The Boston Massacre of March 5, 1770, is depicted in another engraving by Paul Revere. British soldiers clashed with Bostonians who were angered by the Townshend Acts, which placed a tax on paint, paper, lead, and tea. Five colonists, including Crispus Attucks, who is said to be the first black man killed in the struggle for American independence, died in the conflict.

was to become Boston. By 1640, the Massachusetts Bay Colony had about 10,000 people.

Although the Puritans stood for political freedom and a democratic form of government, this attitude did not extend to their religious views. Some religious groups were sent away from the Massachusetts Bay Colony, and others left on their own. Searching for religious freedom, these exiles established settlements in Connecticut in 1635, Rhode Island in 1636, New Hampshire in 1638, and Maine in 1652. Connecticut and Rhode Island became separate colonies, but New Hampshire did not separate from Massachusetts until 1680, and Maine until 1820.

Indian wars plagued Massachusetts until the 1680s. After that the people experienced a relatively peaceful period combined with a quickly growing, mostly agricultural, economy. But many of the early settlers took to the sea for survival, and began to develop commercial fishing to build ships that would carry cargoes all over the world. In 1691 a new charter for Massachusetts combined the colonies of Plymouth and Massachusetts Bay.

Boston became an international port and a center for trade and manufacture, the greatest in New England, and for a time the most important in the colonial world. Fleet sailing vessels, built in the yards of Massachusetts, manned by Yankee captains and crews, developed profitable trade with other lands, particularly the Orient. At the same time, shops and factories multiplied.

During the 1760s there were rumblings of rebellion against the mother country in the Massachusetts Colony. King George III of England had placed a heavy tax on the colonists with his Stamp Act of 1765, and the cry "No taxation without representation" spread throughout the colony. An angry mob in Boston destroyed the British lieutenant governor's house.

Bitterness between the colonists and the British government increased, especially after British Army troops were quartered in Boston. When some of these troops killed several colonists while battling a mob in the Boston Massacre of 1770, a real rebellion began to brew.

In 1773, in protest over the enforcement of a tea tax, a group of Boston citizens staged an uprising. Dressed as Indians, they climbed aboard a British cargo ship in Boston Harbor and dumped 340 chests of tea into the water. This raid became known as the Boston Tea Party.

The first shots in the Revolutionary War were fired in Lexington on April 18, 1775. British troops were marching from Boston to Concord to seize the colonists' hidden supplies of gunpowder. Paul Revere and others made the famous Midnight Ride to warn their fellow colonists. When the British reached Lexington, they were attacked by the minutemen.

At right:
The Battle of Lexington, on April 19, 1775, was the first engagement of the Revolutionary War. Passage by the British parliament of the Intolerable Acts and the quartering of British troops in Boston preceded the armed conflict on the Lexington town green. Eight colonists were killed and 10 wounded before the minutemen retreated and allowed the British to proceed to Concord.

Below:
Bostonian Paul Revere, patriot, engraver, and silversmith, played an important part in events leading up to the Revolutionary War. He participated in the Boston Tea Party of 1773 and served as a liaison between patriot committees in New York and Massachusetts.

Much of the early fighting in the Revolution took place in Massachusetts, whose soldiers fought bravely at Lexington, Concord, and Bunker (actually Breed's) Hill. Then, on July 3, 1775, General George Washington took command of the Continental Army at Cambridge, driving the British out of Boston in the spring of 1776. This was the first major American victory of the war, which Massachusetts supported with men and money until 1783, when peace was declared. On February 6, 1788, Massachusetts accepted the new Constitution of the United States, on the condition that a bill of rights be added to it. It became the sixth state in the Union. The Bill of Rights went into effect on December 15, 1791.

A long embargo and the War of 1812 with Great Britain spurred domestic manufacturing, since world markets were closed to Massachusetts for seven years. In 1814 the first power loom in the United States was installed at Waltham by Francis Cabot Lowell. His textile factory revolutionized the industry. Among the citizens of Massachusetts were able craftsmen and designers. Paul Revere, of

Revolutionary War fame, a silversmith and engraver, was a pioneer in new methods of metalcrafting. The whaling industry flourished in Boston, New Bedford, and Nantucket until the 1860s.

Long before the Civil War, Massachusetts citizens opposed slavery. As early as 1831, editor William Lloyd Garrison was publishing his anti-slavery newspaper, *The Liberator*. Members of the New England Anti-Slavery Society were helping slaves escape to Canada. When the war came, the state furnished more than 125,000 men to the Union Army and about 20,000 to the U.S. Navy, whose first ship had been commissioned at Marblehead in 1775.

After the Civil War, Massachusetts industry expanded still more, and thousands of immigrants poured into the state to work in the textile, shoe, and metal factories. By 1900 Massachusetts's population had swelled to about 2,500,000.

Exploitation of factory workers led to a strike by the textile workers in Lawrence in 1912 and made the public aware of the poor working conditions in the mills. As a result, many improvements were made in American factories and labor-relations policies.

After the United States entered World War I in 1917, the first unit to reach the battlefields of France was Massachusetts's Yankee (26th) Division. During the 1920s the textile and shoe industries in the state suffered from competition from the southern and western states. But industry was on the rise again when the United States entered World War II in 1941. Following World War II many people left the cities for the suburbs. Major cities, such as Boston and Springfield, underwent urban renewal programs. In the mid-1970s, a U.S. court order promoting racial integration of Boston public schools was violently protested by many white Bostonians. This was a rare departure from Boston's liberal politics. Today new industries, including electronics and space and rocket research, are thriving. The Boston metropolitan area alone has dozens of research laboratories. Construction, tourism, and commercial fishing are vital segments of the state's economy.

Above:
Warships docked at Battleship Cove in Fall River. During World Wars I and II, demand for military supplies and equipment turned Massachusetts industry toward durable goods. At the same time, the weakening textile industry moved south, changing the nature of the state's economy.

Below:
The John F. Kennedy Memorial Library in Dorchester is one of the state's most impressive research facilities. Massachusetts has more than 50 colleges and universities with extensive collections, and Boston alone has four outstanding libraries.

Above:
John Hancock, a leader in the struggle for American independence, was a native of Braintree. In 1775 he was elected president of the Continental Congress and, in that capacity, was the first man to sign the Declaration of Independence.

Education

Massachusetts's love for learning was demonstrated at an early date with the establishment of a school by the Puritans in Boston in 1635. In 1642 the colonial government gave each town the responsibility for educating all children whose parents were unable to do so. By 1647 all towns of 50 families or more were ordered to set up elementary schools—the first time anywhere in the world that a government provided free public education at public expense. The first library in the American colonies was established in 1638, at Harvard College, the oldest institution of higher education in the United States. With more than nine million volumes, this is the largest university library in the world. Harvard College was founded in 1636 as a school for training magistrates and clergymen. By 1850 there were nine other colleges and universities in Massachusetts: Williams College (1793), Amherst College (1821), Wheaton College (1834), Mount Holyoke College (1836), Boston University (1839), the Massachusetts State Colleges at Framingham (1839), Westfield (1839), and Bridgewater (1840), and the College of the Holy Cross (1843). Today the state has more than 50 institutions of higher education.

The People

Almost 84 percent of the people in Massachusetts live in cities and towns, including Boston, Springfield, and Worcester; almost 90 percent of them were born in the United States. Most of those born in foreign countries came from Canada, Italy, and Ireland. More than half of the people in the state belong to the Roman Catholic

Above:
Benjamin Franklin, closely associated with Philadelphia, moved there from his native Boston in 1723. Franklin discovered that lightning is electricity and pursued his scientific interests throughout a long career as editor of the *Pennsylvania Gazette* and *Poor Richard's Almanac*. He served as a diplomat to France during the Revolutionary War and was one of the best-known figures of the eighteenth century.

Above:
Lucretia Mott, born to a Quaker family on Nantucket Island, was a leading feminist and reformer during the 19th century.

Below:
Susan B. Anthony, a native of Adams, was the primary organizer of the drive for women's voting rights in America.

Above:
John Adams, the second president of the United States, was born in Braintree (now Quincy). During his term as chief executive, the Library of Congress and the Department of the Navy were established.

Below:
John Quincy Adams, born in Braintree, was the sixth president of the United States. He served as a diplomat before and during his father's administration and was elected president in 1824.

Above:
John Fitzgerald Kennedy, the 35th president of the United States, was born in Brookline. During his presidency, Kennedy established the Peace Corps, forced the Soviet Union to remove its missiles from Cuba, and saw the first American launched into space. He was the youngest man ever elected to the presidency, at the age of 43. Kennedy was assassinated on November 22, 1963, while riding in a motorcade through downtown Dallas, Texas.

Church. The United Church of Christ has the second largest membership, and the Episcopal Church ranks third.

At right:
Edgar Allan Poe, born in Boston, was a poet and short-story writer who focused on themes of the mysterious and the grotesque. *The Raven* is one of his best-known poems, and his chilling stories include *The Masque of the Red Death* and *The Murders in the Rue Morgue*.

Above:
Poet and essayist Ralph Waldo Emerson was a native of Boston. His writing focused on the nature of man, and his *Essays*, published in 1841, are considered a landmark in American literature for their view of human beings as self-sufficient moral and spiritual entities.

Famous People
Many famous people were born in the state of Massachusetts. Here are a few:

Writers
Horatio Alger 1832-1899, Revere. Children's author: *Luck and Pluck*
William Cullen Bryant 1794-1878, Cummington. Poet: "Thanatopsis"
John Cheever 1912-1983, Quincy. Novelist and short story writer: *Bullet Park*
John Ciardi 1916-1986, Boston. Poet: *The Wish Tree*
e. e. cummings 1894-1962, Cambridge. Poet: *95 Poems*
Richard Henry Dana 1815-1882, Cambridge. Novelist: *Two Years Before the Mast*
Emily Dickinson 1830-1886, Amherst. Poet: *Collected Poems*
Ralph Waldo Emerson 1803-1882, Boston. Philosopher, poet, essayist: *Representative Men*

Theodore Geisel, better known as Doctor Seuss, is the creator of a popular series of children's books.

Erle Stanley Gardner 1889-1970, Malden. Mystery writer: the Perry Mason books
Theodore "Doctor Seuss" Geisel 1904-1991, Springfield. Children's author and illustrator: *The Cat in the Hat*
Nathaniel Hawthorne 1806-1864, Salem. Novelist: *The House of Seven Gables*
George V. Higgins b.1939, Brockton. Novelist: *The Friends of Eddie Coyle*
Oliver Wendell Holmes 1809-1894, Cambridge. Physician, poet and essayist: "The Chambered Nautilus"
Helen Hunt Jackson 1830-1885, Amherst. Novelist: *Ramona*
Jack Kerouac 1922-1969, Lowell. Novelist: *On the Road*
Amy Lowell 1874-1925, Brookline. Pulitzer Prize-winning poet: *What's O'Clock*
James Russell Lowell 1819-1891, Cambridge. Poet: *The Vision of Sir Launfal*
Robert Lowell 1917-1977, Boston. Pulitzer Prize-winning poet: *The Dolphin*
William Manchester b.1922, Attleboro. Biographer: *American Caesar*
Robin Moore b. 1925, Concord. Novelist: *The French Connection*
Sylvia Plath 1932-1963, Boston. Poet and novelist: *The Bell Jar*
Edgar Allen Poe 1809-1849, Boston. Poet and short-story writer: "The Fall of the House of Usher"
Laura Elizabeth Richards 1850-1943, Boston.

Pulitzer Prize-winning biographer: *The Life of Julia Ward Howe*

Anne Sexton 1928-1974, Newton. Pulitzer Prize-winning poet: *Live or Die*

Paul Theroux b.1941, Medford. Novelist and essayist: *The Old Patagonian Express, The Mosquito Coast*

John Greenleaf Whittier 1807-1892, Haverhill. Poet: "The Barefoot Boy"

Theodore White was awarded a Pulitzer Prize for his book The Making of the President 1960.

Journalists

Leslie Stahl b.1941, Lynn. TV correspondent

Mike Wallace b.1918, Brookline. TV correspondent

Barbara Walters b.1931, Boston. TV interviewer

Theodore H. White 1915-1986, Boston. Pulitzer Prize-winning journalist

Artists

Charles Bulfinch 1763-1844, Boston. Architect

Daniel Hudson Burnham 1846-1912, Henderson. Architect

John Singleton Copley 1738-1815, Boston. Painter

Nathaniel Currier 1813-1886, Roxbury. Lithographer

Charles Dana Gibson 1867-1944, Roxbury. Artist and illustrator

Childe Hassam 1859-1935, Boston. Impressionist painter

Winslow Homer 1836-1910, Boston. Romantic painter

William Le Baron Jenney 1832-1907, Fairhaven. Architect

Geraldine Farrar sang the title role in Puccini's Madama Butterfly *at the Metropolitan Opera in New York.*

Albert Pinkham Ryder 1847-1917, New Bedford. Painter

James Abbott McNeill Whistler 1834-1903, Lowell. Painter

Classical Musicians

Leonard Bernstein 1918-1990, Lawrence. Composer and conductor

Henry David Thoreau, poet, naturalist, and essayist, is perhaps best known as the writer of Walden.

Geraldine Farrar 1882-1967, Melrose. Operatic soprano

Arthur Fiedler 1894-1979, Boston. Conductor

Philosophers and Religious Leaders

Cotton Mather 1663-1728, Boston. Colonial clergyman

Increase Mather 1639-1723, Dorchester. Colonial clergyman

Dwight L. Moody 1837-1899, East Northfield. Evangelist

Charles S. Peirce 1839-1914, Cambridge. Philosopher

Henry David Thoreau 1817-1862, Concord. Essayist and poet

Scholars

Henry Adams 1838-1918, Boston. Historian and novelist

George Bancroft 1800-1891, Worcester. Historian

John Bartlett 1820-1905, Plymouth. Editor

Granville Stanley Hall 1844-1924, Ashfield. Psychologist

Samuel Eliot Morison 1887-1976, Boston. Naval historian

Educators

Frederick A. Barnard 1809-1889, Sheffield. Founder of Barnard College

Charles W. Eliot 1834-1926, Boston. President of Harvard College

Mark Hopkins 1802-1887, Stockbridge. President of Williams College

Mary Lyon 1797-1849, Buckland. Founder of Mount Holyoke College

Horace Mann 1796-1859, Franklin. Founded the Massachusetts public education system

Elizabeth Palmer Peabody 1804-1894, Billerica. Founder of first U.S. kindergarten

Anne Sullivan 1866-1936, Feeding Hills. Teacher of Helen Keller

Dr. Vannevar Bush built the first analog computer and led the U.S. in early uranium research.

Scientists and Inventors

Percy Williams Bridgman 1882-1961, Cambridge. Nobel Prize-winning physicist

Luther Burbank 1849-1946, Lancaster. Botanist

Vannevar Bush 1890-1974, Everett. Co-founder of the National Science Foundation

Richard Buckminster Fuller 1895-1983, Milton. Engineer and architect. Developer of the geodesic dome

Robert Goddard 1882-1945, Worcester. Father of modern rocketry

Elias Howe 1819-1867, Spencer. Invented the first practical sewing machine

Percival Lowell 1855-1916, Boston. Astronomer

Samuel F. B. Morse 1791-1872, Charlestown. Co-inventor of the first practical telegraph

William Morton 1819-1868, Charlton. Dentist: First to use ether as an anesthetic

Donald MacMillan led numerous expeditions to the Arctic.

Charles B. Sumner 1887-1955, Canton. Nobel Prize-winning biochemist

Eli Whitney 1765-1825, Westborough. Inventor of the cotton gin

Explorer

Donald MacMillan 1874-1970, Provincetown. Arctic explorer

Government Officials

John Adams 1735-1826, Quincy. Second president of the United States

John Quincy Adams 1767-1848, Quincy. Sixth president of the United States

Samuel Adams 1722-1803, Boston. Revolutionary and signer of the Declaration of Independence

Josiah Bartlett 1729-1795, Amesbury. Revolutionary and signer of the Declaration of Independence

George Bush b.1924, Milton. Forty-first president of the United States

Benjamin Franklin 1706-1790, Boston. Diplomat, scientist, inventor, printer, writer, and signer of the Declaration of Independence

Elbridge Gerry 1744-1814, Marblehead. Vice-president under Madison and signer of the Declaration of Independence

John Hancock 1737-1793, Braintree. President of the Continental Congress and first signer of the Declaration of Independence

Oliver Wendell Holmes, Jr. 1841-1945, Boston. U.S. Supreme Court justice

Edward M. Kennedy b.1932, Brookline. U.S. senator

John F. Kennedy 1917-1963, Brookline. Thirty-fifth president of the United States

Robert F. Kennedy 1925-1968, Brookline. U.S. attorney general and senator

William L. Marcy 1786-1857, Southbridge. U.S. senator, secretary of war, and secretary of state

Frances Perkins 1882-1965, Boston. Secretary of labor under Franklin D. Roosevelt: First woman cabinet member

Elliott Richardson b.1920, Boston. U.S. Secretary of defense, secretary of Health, Education, and Welfare, attorney general and ambassador to Great Britain

Joseph Story 1779-1845, Marblehead. U.S. Supreme Court justice

Robert F. Kennedy, attorney general in the Kennedy administration, was assassinated during the 1968 presidential campaign.

Military Figures

Crispus Attucks 1723-1770, Framingham. Revolutionary: Killed in the Boston Massacre

Joseph Hooker 1814-1879, Hadley. Union general

Arthur MacArthur 1845-1912, Chicopee Falls. Spanish-American War general

Nelson Miles 1839-1925, Westminster. Indian Wars general

David Porter 1780-1843, Boston. War of 1812 commodore

Israel Putnam 1718-1790, Salem Village. Revolutionary War general

Paul Revere 1735-1818, Boston. Silversmith, famed for his ride to Concord to warn of the approach of the British

Joseph Warren 1741-1775, Roxbury. Physician and Revolutionary War general

Social Reformers

Susan B. Anthony 1820-1906, Adams. Crusader for women suffrage

Emily Green Balch 1867-1961, Boston. Nobel Prize-winning pacifist

Clara Barton 1821-1912, Oxford. Founder of the American Red Cross

W. E. B. DuBois 1868-1963, Great Barrington. Civil rights leader
William Lloyd Garrison 1805-1879, Newburyport. Abolitionist journalist
Samuel Howe 1801-1876, Boston. Director of Perkins School for the Blind and founder of first U.S. school for the mentally retarded
Lucretia Mott 1793-1880, Nantucket. Abolitionist and feminist
Lucy Stone 1818-1893, West Brookfield. Abolitionist and feminist

Business Leaders
Erastus B. Bigelow 1814-1879, West Boylston. Founder of Bigelow carpet mills
John H. Breck 1877-1965, Holyoke. Cosmetics manufacturer
Thomas C. Durant 1820-1885, Lee. Organizer of the Union Pacific Railroad
William C. Durant 1861-1947, Boston. Automobile manufacturer

W. E. B. Du Bois, a distinguished scholar, was one of the founders of the NAACP.

Cyrus Field 1819-1892, Stockbridge. Laid the first transatlantic cable
Marshall Field 1834-1906, Conway. Department store founder
Edward A. Filene 1860-1937, Salem. Department store founder
Herbert T. Kalmus 1881-1963, Chelsea. Co-developer of Technicolor
Joseph P. Kennedy 1888-1969, Boston. Financier and ambassador to Great Britain
Abbott Lawrence 1792-1855, Groton. Manufacturer and ambassador to Great Britain
James S. Love 1896-1962, Cambridge. Textile executive. Founder of Burlington Industries
George S. Parker 1866-1952, Salem. Founder of Parker Brothers, manufacturer of board games
Charles Pratt 1830-1892, Watertown. Oilman and founder of Pratt Institute
Charles H. Revson 1906-1975, Boston. Founder of Revlon cosmetics company
Gustavus F. Swift 1839-1903, Sandwich. Incorporated Swift and Co. meat packing company
J. Walter Thompson 1847-1928, Pittsfield. Advertising executive

Sports Personalities
Tenley Albright b.1935, Newton Center. Olympic goal medal-winning figure skater

Bette Davis as she appeared in the 1950 film All About Eve.

Leo Durocher 1906-1991, West Springfield. Baseball player and manager

A. Bartlett Giamatti 1938-1989, Boston. Commissioner of baseball

Connie Mack 1862-1956, East Brookfield. Baseball manager

Rocky Marciano 1923-1969, Brockton. World heavyweight boxing champion

John L. Sullivan 1858-1918, Boston. World heavyweight boxing champion

Entertainers

Jack Albertson 1910-1981, Malden. Academy Award-winning actor: *The Subject Was Roses*

Jane Alexander b.1939, Boston. Tony Award-winning actress: *The Great White Hope*

Walter Brennan 1894-1974, Lynn. Three-time Academy Award-winning actor: *The Westerner*

Bette Davis 1908-1989, Lowell. Two-time Academy Award-winning actress: *Jezebel*

Ruth Gordon 1896-1985, Wollaston. Playwright and Academy Award-winning actress: *Rosemary's Baby*

Madeline Kahn b.1942, Boston. Film actress: *Young Frankenstein*

Jack Lemmon b.1925, Boston. Two-time Academy Award-winning actor: *Save the Tiger*

Dorothy Loudon b.1933, Boston. Tony Award-winning actress: *Annie*

Robert Morse b.1931, Newton. Tony Award-winning actor: *How to Succeed in Business Without Really Trying*

Barry Newman b.1938, Boston. Emmy Award-winning actor: *Petrocelli*

Leonard Nimoy b.1931, Boston. Television actor: *Star Trek*

Robert Preston 1918-1987,

Ruth Gordon was well known both as an actress and author of several plays and screenplays.

Newton Highlands. Film actor: *The Music Man*

Lee Remick 1935-1991, Boston. Film actress: *The Omen*

Other Personalities

Abigail Adams 1744-1818, Weymouth. Wife of John Adams and writer

F. Lee Bailey b.1933, Waltham. Criminal lawyer: represented Patty Hearst

John "Johnny Appleseed" Chapman 1774-1845, Leominster. Conservationist: Planted many apple nurseries from the Alleghenies to Ohio and beyond

Fannie Farmer 1857-1915, Boston. Founder of Miss Farmer's School of Cookery and author of cookbooks

Singers

Donna Summer b.1948, Boston. Disco singer

James Taylor b.1948, Boston. Pop singer

Cecil B. DeMille won an Academy Award for Best Picture in 1952 for The Greatest Show on Earth.

Dancers

Ray Bolger 1904-1987, Boston. Film dancer: *The Wizard of Oz*

Eleanor Powell 1912-1982, Springfield. Film dancer: *Rosalie*

Directors

Cecil B. DeMille 1881-1959, Ashfield. Academy Award-winning director: *The Greatest Show on Earth*

William Wellman 1896-1975, Brookline. Academy Award-winning director: *A Star Is Born*

Colleges and Universities

There are many colleges and universities in Massachusetts. Here are the more prominent, with their locations, dates of founding, and enrollment.

American International College, Springfield, 1885, 1,831

Amherst College, Amherst, 1821, 1,580

Anna Maria College for Men and Women, Paxton, 1946, 1,447

Assumption College, Worcester, 1904, 2,974

Atlantic Union College, South Lancaster, 1882, 1,228

Babson College, Wellesley, 1919, 3,040

Berklee College of Music, Boston, 1945, 2,734

Boston College, Chestnut Hill, 1863, 14,515

Boston Conservatory, Boston, 1867, 387

Boston University, Boston, 1839, 24,071

Brandeis University, Waltham, 1948, 3,793

Bridgewater State College, Bridgewater, 1840, 5,299

Clark University, Worcester, 1887, 2,909

College of the Holy Cross, Worcester, 1843, 2,738

Eastern Nazarene College, Quincy, 1918, 919

Emerson College, Boston, 1880, 2,423

Emmanuel College, Boston, 1919, 1,205

Fitchburg State College, Fitchburg, 1894, 6,179

Gordon College, Wenham, 1889, 1,150

Hampshire College, Amherst, 1965, 1,263

Harvard University, Cambridge, 1636, 18,273

Lesley College, Cambridge, 1909, 5,500

Massachusetts College of Pharmacy and Allied Health Sciences, Boston, 1823, 1,136

Massachusetts Institute of Technology, Cambridge, 1861, 9,628

Merrimack College, North Andover, 1947, 2,395

Mount Holyoke College, South Hadley, 1837, 1,879

New England Conservatory of Music, Boston, 1867, 718

North Adams State College, North Adams, 1894, 2,341

Northeastern University, Boston, 1898, 30,515

Regis College, Weston, 1927, 1,163

Salem State College, Salem, 1854, 8,407

Simmons College, Boston, 1899, 2,819

Smith College, Northampton, 1871, 2,765

Springfield College, Springfield, 1885, 3,148

Stonehill College, North Easton, 1948, 1,964

Suffolk University, Boston, 1906, 5,733

Tufts University, Medford, 1852, 7,634

University of Massachusetts at Amherst, 1863, 23,000; *at Boston,* 1964, 11,018

Wellesley College, Wellesley, 1875, 2,279

Westfield State College, Westfield, 1838, 5,292

Wheaton College, Norton, 1834, 1,264

Wheelock College, Boston, 1888, 1,208

Williams College, Williamstown, 1793, 2,120

Worcester Polytechnic Institute, Worcester, 1865, 3,892

Worcester State College, Worcester, 1874, 5,246

Where To Get More Information

Massachusetts Department of Commerce and Development
Division of Tourism
100 Cambridge Street, 13th Floor
Boston, MA 02202
617-536-4100
617-727-3201

Rhode Island

In 1647, the Rhode Island Colony adopted a seal—an anchor. In 1664, the motto *Hope* was added. The present state seal was adopted in 1875. It is round, and in the center is the anchor. Above the anchor is the state motto. Around the outer edge of the circle are the words *Seal of the State of Rhode Island and Providence Plantations* and the date 1636, the year of the founding of Providence, the state's first settlement.

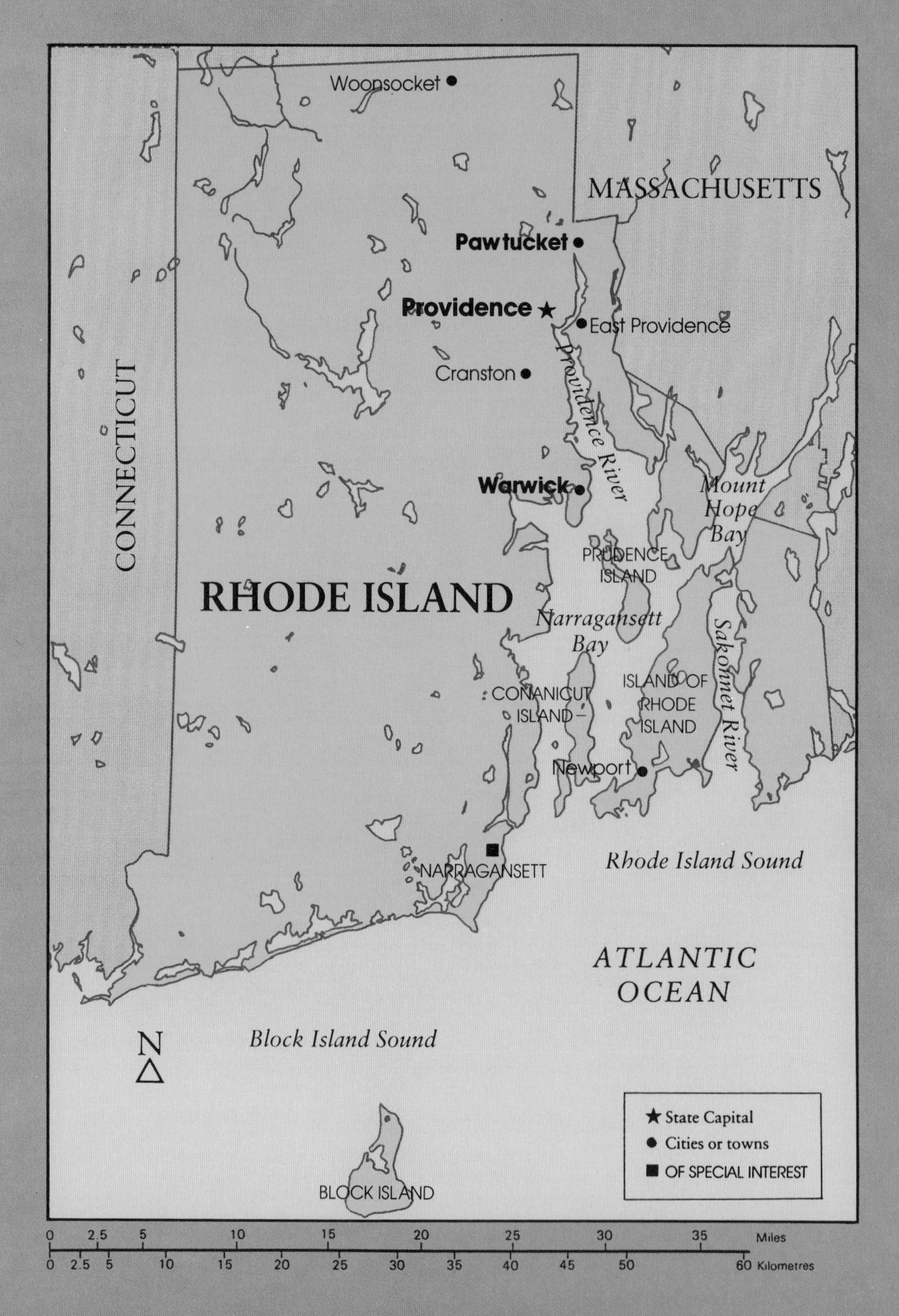

State Flower: Violet

State Flag

State Motto: Hope

State Tree: Red Maple

State Song: "Rhode Island"

RHODE ISLAND

At a Glance

Capital: Providence

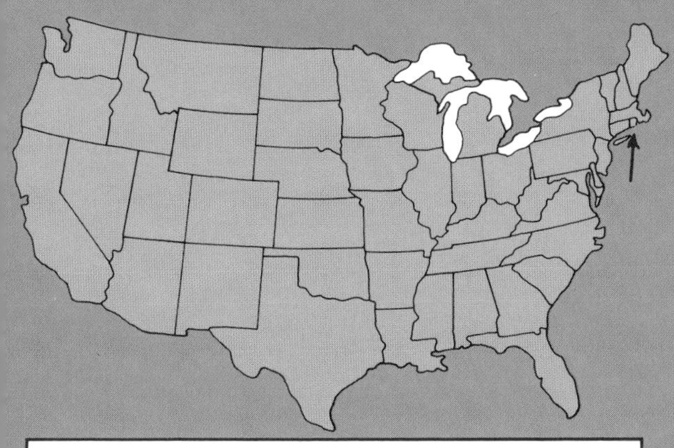

Size: 1,212 square miles (smallest)
Population: 1,005,091 (43rd largest)

Major Industries: Textiles, electronics, silverware, agriculture

Major Crops: Potatoes, apples, corn

State Bird: Rhode Island Red Chicken

State Flag

The state flag was adopted in 1877. On a white field, symbolizing the white uniforms worn by Rhode Island soldiers in the Revolutionary War, is a golden anchor. Under the anchor, on a blue scroll, is the state motto. Thirteen gold stars, representing the 13 original colonies, form a circle around the anchor and motto.

State Motto

Hope

This simple motto was adopted in 1664.

Boats come from all over to take part in Newport's many harbor festivals.

State Capital

From 1663 to 1854, Rhode Island had five capitals at the same time—Newport, East Greenwich, Bristol, South Kingstown, and Providence. From 1854 to 1900 there were only two—Newport and Providence. Finally, in 1900, Providence was made the sole capital of the state.

State Name and Nicknames

There are two theories about how Rhode Island was named: One says that it was Giovanni da Verrazano, an Italian explorer sponsored by France, who, in 1524, noticed that the area resembled the Island of Rhodes in the Mediterranean Sea. The other theory claims that in 1614 the Dutch explorer Adriaen Block called an island in Narragansett Bay *Roodt Eylandt*, or "Red Island." Actually, the complete official name of the state is "The State of Rhode Island and Providence Plantations."

Rhode Island has several nicknames. Because it is the smallest of the 50 states, it is sometimes called "Little Rhody." However, the preferred name is the "Ocean State" because of its coastline.

State Flower

Adopted in 1968, the violet, *Viola palmata*, is the state flower of Rhode Island. It is also called the early blue violet and the Johnny-jump-up.

State Tree

Acer rubrum, the red maple, was named the state tree in 1964. It is also called the soft maple, the water maple, the scarlet maple, the white maple, the swamp maple, and the shoe-peg maple.

State Bird

The Rhode Island Red, a breed of domestic chicken, was named the state bird in 1954.

State American Folk Art Symbol

The Charles I. D. Looff Carousel was named the state American folk art symbol in 1985.

State Mineral

Bowenite was adopted as the state mineral in 1966.

State Rock

Cumberlandite was named the state rock in 1966.

State Song

In 1946, "Rhode Island," by T. Clarke Brown, was adopted as the state song.

Population

The population of Rhode Island in 1992 was 1,005,091, making it the 43rd most populous state. There are 961.8 people per square mile.

Industry

The principal industries of the state are services, tourism and manufacturing. The chief products are costume jewelry, machinery, textiles, electronics, and silverware.

Agriculture

The chief crops of the state are nursery products, turf, potatoes, and apples. Rhode Island is also a livestock state, and there are estimated to be 7,000 cattle; 6,400 hogs and pigs; 6,500 sheep; and 430,000 chickens, geese, and turkeys on its farms. Oak and chestnut timber is harvested, and sand, gravel, and crushed stone are important mineral resources. Commercial fishing, especially for lobster and other shellfish, earned $85.7 million in 1992.

Government

The governor is elected to a two-year term, as are the lieutenant governor, the attorney general, the secretary of state, and the state treasurer. The state legislature, called the general assembly, which meets annually, consists of a 50-member senate and a 100-member house of representatives. A city has one senator for each 25,000 registered voters. Voters in cities and towns elect from one to 25 representatives, depending on their populations. The state constitution was adopted in 1842. In addition to its two U.S. senators, Rhode Island has two representatives in the U.S. House of Representatives. The state has four votes in the electoral college.

Sports

Many sporting events on the collegiate and secondary school levels are played all over the state. The first United States men's tennis championships were played in Newport in 1881, which still hosts an invitational tennis tournament. The Basque sport of jai alai is played in Newport. Sailing and fishing in Narragansett Bay and in the Atlantic Ocean are other popular pastimes.

The Tennis Hall of Fame and Tennis Museum in Newport was the site of the first National Singles Championship.

Major Cities

Newport (population 28,227). Settled in 1639, Newport was the site of the first school in Rhode Island, which opened the following year. Shipbuilding began in 1646, and the city's fame as a summer resort began shortly after the Civil War.

Places to visit in Newport:
The Touro Synagogue (1763), the Newport Historical Society Museum, many opulent mansions, including The Breakers (1895), Rosecliff (1902), and Marble House (1892), the Wanton-Lyman House (1675), the Artillery Company of Newport Museum, the Old Stone Mill, the Brick Market (1762), the Old Colony House (1739), the International Tennis Hall of Fame and Tennis Museum, the Redwood Library (1748), Trinity Church (1726), the Samuel Whitehorne House (1811), the Friends Meeting House (1699), the Whitehall Museum House (1729), and Hammersmith Farm (1887).

Providence (population 160,782). Settled in 1636, the state capital is home to about one-third of the state's population. Providence started as a farm center, and when it began its great maritime history in the 18th century, it soon became a major port and shipbuilding town. The city is now a prominent silverware and jewelry producer, and also manufactures machine tools, hardware, and oil and rubber products.

Places to visit in Providence:
The State House, the First Baptist Church in America (1775), the Old State House,

Newport is located on Aquidneck Island in the mouth of Rhode Island's Narragansett Bay.

Cathedral of Saint John the Divine (1810), the Providence Art Club, the Providence Athenaeum (1753), the Governor Stephen Hopkins House (1707), the Museum of Rhode Island History at Aldrich House, the First Unitarian Church (1816), the John Brown House (1786), the Arcade (1828), the Davol Square Marketplace, Roger Williams National Memorial, the North Burial Ground, Brown University, and the Rhode Island School of Design.

Places To Visit

The National Park Service maintains two areas in Rhode Island. They are the Roger Williams National Memorial and the Touro Synagogue National Historic Site. In addition, there are 18 state recreation areas.

Block Island: Monhegan Cliffs. Clay cliffs rise to a height of 200 feet, near the lighthouse on this popular island.

Bristol: Herreshoff Marine Museum.

East Greenwich: General James Mitchell Varnum House. Built in 1773, this house furnished with period furniture was once the home of the Revolutionary War officer.

Jamestown: Watson Farm. Dating from 1796, this working farm has 285 acres.

Narragansett: The Towers. This building is all that remains of a 19th-century casino designed by Stanford White.

Pawtucket: Slater Mill Historic Site. The site contains the Old Slater Mill (1793), the Wilkinson Mill (1810), and the Sylvanus Brown House (1758), all depicting factory production and life in a 19th-century industrial village.

Tiverton: Fort Barton. This fort was the staging point for 11,000 British troops during the Revolution.

Events

Here are some of the events scheduled in Rhode Island.

Sports: Mid-Winter New England Surfing Championship (Newport), A Weekend of Coaching (Newport), Wooden Boat Show and Classic Yacht Regatta (Newport), International Horse Jumping Derby (Portsmouth), Greyhound racing at Lincoln Greyhound Park (Providence).

Arts and Crafts: Summer Festival (East Greenwich), Wickford Art Festival (North Kingston).

Music: Music Festival (Newport), JVC Jazz Festival (Newport), Blackstone Valley Summer Music Festival (Pawtucket), Rhode Island Philharmonic (Providence).

Entertainment: Harvest Fair (Bristol), Hot Air Balloon Festival (Kingston), Newport Irish Heritage Month (Newport), Quonset International Air Show and Exposition (North Kingston).

Tours: Spring Festival of Historic Houses (Providence).

Theater: Theatre-by-the-Sea (Charlestown), Trinity Repertory Co. (Providence).

The Towers at Narragansett.

Newport Harbor, on Narragansett Bay, is one of the state's best sheltered harbors.

The Land and the Climate

Rhode Island is in the southern tier of the New England states. Its neighbors are, on the north and east, Massachusetts, and on the west, Connecticut. To the south is the open sea, to which Rhode Island has access by Narragansett Bay, one of the great harbors of the world. Rhode Island has two main land regions: the Coastal Lowlands and the Eastern New England Upland.

The Coastal Lowlands comprise more than half the mainland and include the islands in Narragansett Bay and the land east of the bay. This is part of the same land region that covers the entire coastline of the New England states. Rocky cliffs, sandy shores, and rugged, forested hills are typical of this area. It is a region of dairy, vegetable, fruit, hay, and poultry farms.

Above:
Water is Rhode Island's most striking physical feature. The state's many beaches and shoreline resorts are the basis of a strong tourist industry.

At left:
Rhode Island has almost 400 miles of shoreline. Fishing is an important industry, with northern lobsters and hardshell clams accounting for almost 55 percent of the total catch.

The Roger Williams State Park, near Providence, contains some of Rhode Island's most impressive gardens. The state's temperate climate permits the growth of a surprisingly wide range of plants, including 36 varieties of orchid. More than 60 kinds of trees thrive in Rhode Island, including ash, oak, hickory, birch, cedar, and elm.

The Eastern New England Upland, in the northwestern one-third of the state, is part of a region that extends from Maine to Connecticut. It is rough and hilly, dotted with ponds, and includes 812-foot Jerimoth Hill, the highest point in Rhode Island. Fruit, hay, poultry, and dairy cattle are raised here.

The coastline of Rhode Island is 40 miles long, but when the shorelines of the bays and islands are included, it measures 384 miles. The major rivers of the state are the Providence, the Sakonnet, the Seekonk, the Pawtuxet, and the Potowomut.

Rhode Island's climate is milder than is typical throughout New England. Its proximity to Narragansett Bay tempers the weather with warm sea winds. The state has approximately 40 inches of annual rainfall, well distributed through the year. Winter snowfalls are not usually heavy. The range of temperature varies about 10 degrees Fahrenheit throughout the state, with Providence having a January average of 29 degrees F. and a July average of 72 degrees F. This coastal state is subject to occasional hurricanes and flood tides.

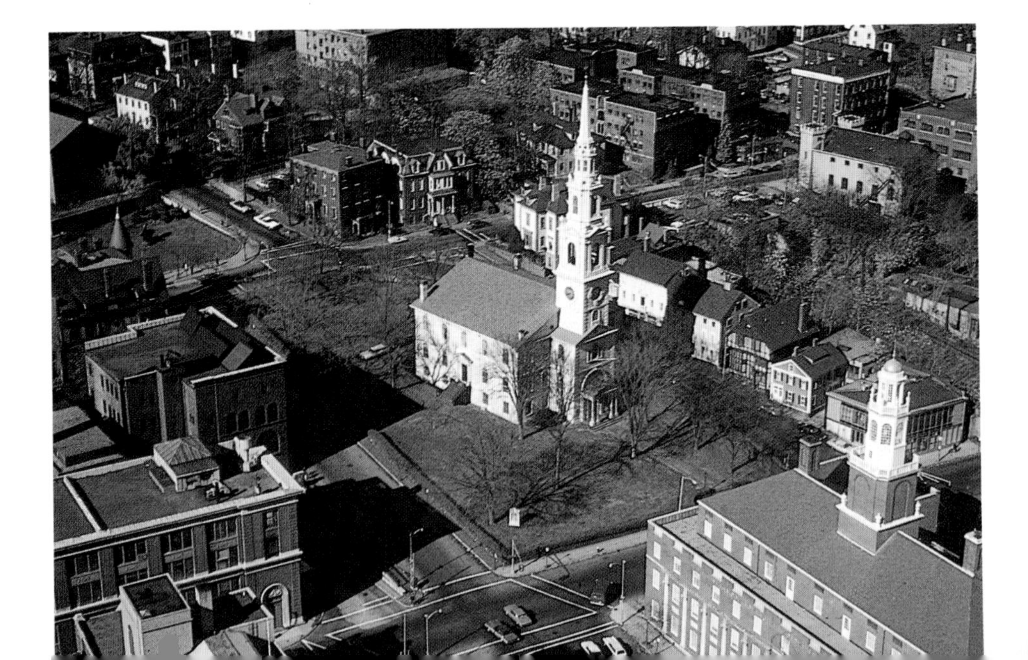

The first Baptist Meeting House in America was founded in Providence, Rhode Island's capital city, in 1775. Providence offered a haven to Jews, Quakers, and others who were unwelcome elsewhere in the American colonies.

The History

Before Europeans came to what is now Rhode Island, several thousand Indians lived there. These Indians belonged to five tribes of the Algonquian family: the Narraganset, Niantic, Nipmuck, Pequot, and Wampanoag. The most populous tribe was the Narraganset, who were peaceful hunters, fishermen, and farmers.

Perhaps the first explorer to see Rhode Island was Miguel de Cortereal, a Portuguese navigator, who may have sailed along the coast in 1511. But certainly Giovanni da Verrazano, an Italian navigator working for France, arrived there in 1524: he reported on his exploration of Narragansett Bay. Some historians believe that he was the person who named the region, since he wrote that it resembled the Greek island of Rhodes in the Mediterranean Sea. Other historians credit the Dutch navigator Adriaen Block, who, in 1614, named an island in Narragansett Bay *Roodt Eylandt*—Red Island—for the bright red clay of its shores.

Colonization of the Rhode Island territory did not occur until Roger Williams, a minister banished from the Massachusetts Bay Colony because he sought religious freedom, migrated south in 1636. Williams selected the site he called Providence for his settlement, after he had bought the land from two Narraganset Indian chiefs, Canonicus and Miantonomo. In 1638 three other refugees from Massachusetts's repressive Puritan regime founded the settlement of Pocasset on Aquidneck Island: Anne Hutchinson, William Coddington, and John Clarke, with their followers. When religious and political differences arose, Anne Hutchinson and her followers stayed at Pocasset, renaming it Portsmouth, while the Coddington and Clarke groups moved south and founded Newport in 1639.

In 1643 Samuel Gorton, John Greene, and others left Providence and settled at Warwick. They had wanted to live under a system of English law, and Providence was largely independent of that system.

Roger Williams, who founded Providence in 1636, was a minister who had been banished from Puritan Massachusetts for "spreading new and dangerous opinions against authority." In search of greater religious and political freedom, Williams came to the Narragansett Bay area, where he bought land from the Indians and established a settlement.

But the move was a peaceful one, and Roger Williams proposed a merger of the four Rhode Island settlements, which was effected under a royal charter in 1647. In 1663 King Charles II of England granted another charter, called the Charter of Rhode Island and Providence Plantations, which remained the law of Rhode Island until 1843. Because of the title of this charter, Rhode Island's official name is still the State of Rhode Island and Providence Plantations—the smallest state has the longest name.

The unique religious freedom that Williams maintained in Rhode Island attracted settlers who were unwelcome in most of the colonies, including Quakers and Jews, primarily from England and Holland. As a result, the Touro Synagogue in Newport, one of the most historic and beautiful buildings in the state, is the oldest Jewish house of worship in the country. Williams also respected the rights of the Indians and sought peaceful relations with them, although Rhode Island was drawn into King Philip's War in 1675, when the Wampanoag chief King Philip (Metacomet) attacked New England colonists to protect tribal lands in Massachusetts. The Indian leader was killed near Mount Hope (present-day Bristol) the following year by colonial forces.

Touro Synagogue, founded in Newport in 1763, is the oldest Jewish house of worship in the country. Roger Williams's policy of religious tolerance prevailed among all four of the settlements that united to form the Rhode Island Colony in 1647.

A 1750 view of Newport from the southwest. The well-protected harbors and bays around the city made it a major seafaring center in the early 1700s.

Rhode Island boomed during the early 1700s. Shipbuilding and seafaring activities based around the well-protected Narragansett Bay predominated. Newport became a big seaport, whose captains sailed to Africa and the West Indies in the "triangle trade": rum, black slaves, and molasses. But in spite of the profitable slave trade, and extensive use of slaves on its prosperous plantations, Rhode Island was the first colony to prohibit the importation of slaves, in 1774.

Rhode Island colonists were among the first to take action against the British when the Revolutionary War began. In fact, they had

burned the British ship *Liberty* at Newport in 1769—six years before hostilities broke out. Hundreds of Rhode Islanders joined the patriot forces: Stephen Hopkins was one of the chief organizers of the Continental Navy and Nathanael Greene won renown as a general. Newport was occupied by the British from December 1776 to October 1779. In May 1776, Rhode Island had become the first colony to declare its independence from Great Britain. It became the last of the 13 original colonies to join the new Union as a state in 1790, when the Bill of Rights was added to the Constitution.

Industrial growth in Rhode Island began after the war with the establishment of the first machine-powered cotton mill in the United States in 1790. In 1794 Nehemiah Dodge of Providence developed a process for plating inexpensive metals with precious metals and began the American jewelry industry. Commercial fishing and whaling were important sources of revenue.

As late as the mid-1800s, more than 95 percent of the people in Rhode Island were of British stock. Then the state's industrial boom began to attract immigrants from other countries to work in the new mills and factories. One large group was Italian and another was French-Canadian. The Canadians established French-speaking districts and sent their children to French schools—most of them in or near Woonsocket. Large numbers of Irish came, followed by

The Slater Mill, on the Blackstone River at Pawtucket, was built by Samuel Slater in 1793 to house the nation's first textile machines, which he developed from British prototypes.

Poles, and, still later, by Portuguese immigrants. Syrians emigrated from the Middle East to work in the textile mills, because they were skilled in the weaving of damask—richly patterned fabrics used for table linen and drapery.

More than 24,000 Rhode Islanders served in the Union Army and Navy during the Civil War, including General Ambrose E. Burnside, who later served as governor of the state. After the war, prosperity continued. When the United States entered World War I in 1917, about 28,000 Rhode Islanders joined the armed forces, and the state's factories made chemicals, munitions, and other war materials. Newport and Providence built ships.

The textile industry in Rhode Island suffered hard times during the 1920s, because many factories were moving south, where labor was cheaper. But the machine-tool, metal-products, and machinery industries were thriving. When the United States entered World War II in 1941, about 93,000 Rhode Island men and women served in the armed forces. Defense plants turned out quantities of war materials, and dozens of combat and cargo ships were launched from Providence. Today, Rhode Island has a varied economy. Industry has continued to diversify, and tourism is on the upswing.

The Old Colony House in Newport, built in 1739, was the meeting place for Rhode Island's General Assembly from 1790 to 1900.

Education

Education has always been important to Rhode Islanders. In colonial times, ministers established schools to teach older boys, and "dame schools" were founded by women to teach younger boys and girls. The people of Newport set up a free school for children of the poor in 1640. A law establishing public schools statewide was enacted in 1800. Rhode Island's first library was established in Newport in 1700, and the first institution of higher education in the state—Brown University—was founded in 1764.

Providence, Rhode Island's oldest and largest city, has a population of more than 150,000.

One of America's foremost portrait painters, Gilbert Stuart, was born near Newport in 1775 and began to paint when he was 13. His work was commissioned by prominent statesmen and society leaders, and he is best known for his many portraits of George Washington.

The People

About 87 percent of the people in Rhode Island live in cities and towns such as Providence. Roughly 90 percent of Rhode Islanders were born in the United States. The largest religious body in the state is made up of Roman Catholics. Other large religious groups include Baptists, Episcopalians, Jews, Lutherans, Methodists, and members of the United Church of Christ.

Famous People
Many famous people were born in the state of Rhode Island. Here are a few:

Writers
H. P. Lovecraft 1890-1937, Providence. Science-fiction writer: *The Dunwich Horror*
Edwin O'Connor 1918-1968, Providence. Novelist: *The Last Hurrah*

Artists
Raymond Mathewson Hood 1881-1934, Pawtucket. Architect
Gilbert Stuart 1755-1828, North Kingstown. Portrait painter

Explorer
Robert Gray 1755-1806, Tiverton. Captain of the first U.S. vessel to circumnavigate the globe

Government Official
Stephen Hopkins 1707-1785, Scituate. Governor and signer of the Declaration of Independence

Military Figures
Nathanael Green 1742-1786, Warwick. Revolutionary War general
Esek Hopkins 1718-1802, Scituate. Revolutionary War naval commander
Matthew Perry 1794-1858, Newport. Mexican War naval commander; led mission to Japan in 1852
Oliver Hazard Perry 1785-1819, South Kingston. Naval captain of the War of 1812

Sports Personality
Napoleon Lajoie 1875-1959, Woonsocket. Hall of Fame baseball player

Entertainers
George M. Cohan 1878-1942, Providence. Actor-songwriter and producer
David Hartman b.1935, Pawtucket. Actor and television host
Van Johnson b.1916, Newport. Film actor: *Command Decision, The Caine Mutiny*

Singer
Nelson Eddy 1901-1967, Providence. Singer-actor: *Rose Marie*

Colleges and Universities
There are only a few colleges and universities in Rhode Island. Here are the more prominent, with their locations dates of founding, and enrollments.

Brown University, Providence, 1764, 7,577
Providence College, Providence, 1917, 5,917
Rhode Island College, Providence, 1854, 9,233
Rhode Island School of Design, Providence, 1877, 1,912
University of Rhode Island, Kingston, 1888, 12,111

Where To Get More Information
Rhode Island Department of Economic Development
Tourism/Promotion Division
7 Jackson Walkway
Providence, RI 02903
1-800-556-2484

Further Reading

General

Aylesworth, Thomas G., and Virginia L. *Let's Discover the States: Southern New England*. New York: Chelsea House Publishers, 1988.

Connecticut

Fradin, Dennis B. *The Connecticut Colony*. Chicago: Childrens Press, 1990.

Kent, Deborah. *America the Beautiful: Connecticut*. Chicago: Childrens Press, 1989.

Roth, David M. *Connecticut: A Bicentennial History*. New York: Norton, 1979.

Roth, David M. *Connecticut, A History*. New York: Norton, 1985.

Sonderlind, Arthur E. *Colonial Connecticut*. Nashville, Tennessee: Nelson, 1976.

Thompson, Kathleen. *Connecticut*. Milwaukee, WI: Raintree Publishers, 1986.

Trumbull, Benjamin. *A Complete History of Connecticut*. New York: Arno Press, 1972.

Massachusetts

Brown, Richard D. *Massachusetts: A Bicentennial History*. New York: Norton, 1978.

Fradin, Dennis B. *The Massachusetts Colony*. Chicago: Childrens Press, 1986.

Kent, Deborah. *America the Beautiful: Massachusetts*. Chicago: Childrens Press, 1987.

Massachusetts: A Guide to the Pilgrim State, 2nd ed. Boston: Houghton Mifflin, 1971.

Whitehill, Walter M., & Norman Korker. *Massachusetts: A Pictorial History*. New York: Scribner's, 1976.

Rhode Island

Alderman, Clifford L. *The Rhode Island Colony*. New York: Macmillan, 1969.

Bailey, Bernadine. *Picture Book of Rhode Island*, rev. ed. Chicago: Whitman, 1971.

Carpenter, Allan. *Rhode Island*. Rev. ed. Chicago: Childrens Press, 1978.

Heinrichs, Ann. *America the Beautiful: Rhode Island*. Chicago: Childrens Press, 1990.

McLoughlin, Warren G. *Rhode Island: A Bicentennial History*. New York: Norton, 1978.

McLoughlin, Warren G. *Rhode Island: A History*. New York: Norton, 1985.

Steinberg, Shelia, and Cathleen McGuigan. *Rhode Island: An Historical Guide*. Providence: Rhode Island Bicentennial Foundation, 1976.

Numbers in italics refer to illustrations

Picture Credits

AP/Wide World Photos: pp. 28, 29, 30, 31, 62, 63, 64, 65, 66, 67, 68, 69; Courtesy of Connecticut Department of Economic Development: pp. 3 (top), 6-7, 11, 12, 15, 16, 17, 18, 19, 25, 27 (right); Bruce Glassman: p. 20; Jill Heisler: pp. 8-9; James Kersell: p. 10; Library of Congress: p. 86; Courtesy of Massachusetts Division of Tourism: pp. 3 (bottom), 34-35, 36-37, 40, 41, 42, 43, 44, 45, 46-47, 48, 49, 50, 51 (bottom), 52, 57; National Portrait Gallery/Smithsonian Institution: pp. 21, 22, 24, 26, 27 (left), 58, 59, 60, 61, 92; New York Public Library/Stokes Collection: pp. 23, 53, 54, 56, 88-89, 90, 91; Courtesy of Old Sturbridge Village: p. 51 (top left and right); Courtesy of Rhode Island Tourism Division: pp. 4, 72-73, 74-75, 77, 78, 79, 80, 81, 82-83, 84, 87.
Cover photos courtesy of Massachusetts Division of Tourism and Rhode Island Tourism Division.